THE FOWRE HYMNES

EDMUND SPENSER

THE FOWRE HYMNES

Edited by

LILIAN WINSTANLEY, M.A.

Late Scholar and Fellow of the Victoria University of Manchester,
Lecturer in English in the University College of Wales, Aberystwyth.

CAMBRIDGE:
at the University Press
1930

CAMBRIDGE
UNIVERSITY PRESS

University Printing House, Cambridge CB2 8BS, United Kingdom

Published in the United States of America by Cambridge University Press, New York

Cambridge University Press is part of the University of Cambridge.

It furthers the University's mission by disseminating knowledge in the pursuit of
education, learning and research at the highest international levels of excellence.

www.cambridge.org
Information on this title: www.cambridge.org/9781107669765

© Cambridge University Press 1907

First edition 1907
First published 1907
Reprinted 1916, 1930
First paperback edition 2014

A catalogue record for this publication is available from the British Library

ISBN 978-1-107-66976-5 Paperback

PREFACE.

THIS edition of Spenser's *Fowre Hymnes* is intended mainly for the use of students and, since it has not been possible to assume in all cases a knowledge of the original languages, the writer has employed Jowett's translations of the *Phaedrus* and *Symposium* and has made either translations or summaries of the passages quoted from Ficino's *Commentarium in Convivium* and Bruno's *De gl' Heroici Furori*. Though the work is intended primarily for students it is hoped that the Introduction may prove of some use to Spenserian scholars generally; so far as the editor knows the influence of the *Heroici Furori* on Spenser has not been suggested before and that of the *Symposium* and *Phaedrus* and of Ficino is worked out much more fully than can be found elsewhere.

Students who wish to pursue the subject in Spenser's contemporaries are referred to Mr Harrison's excellent monograph on *Platonism in English Poetry*.

L. WINSTANLEY.

September, 1907.

CONTENTS.

                                                                        PAGES

INTRODUCTION . . . . ix—lxxii

   I.   Spenser and Plato . . . . . . ix—xxviii

  II. The Influence of Plato on the *Fowre Hymnes* . xxviii—lvii

 III. The Influence of Ficino and Bruno on the
         Fowre Hymnes . . . . . . lviii—lxxii

THE FOWRE HYMNES . . . . 1—41

  An Hymne in Honour of Love . . . . 2—11

  An Hymne in Honour of Beautie . . . 12—21

  An Hymne of Heavenly Love . . . . 22—31

  An Hymne of Heavenly Beautie . . . 32—41

NOTES . . . . 43—76

INDEX . . . . 77—79

INTRODUCTION.

I.

SPENSER AND PLATO.

IN estimating the place of the *Fowre Hymnes* in Spenser's work it is important to bear in mind that they represent in its clearest form that Platonism which was, throughout his life, one of his chief inspirations. No English poet, with the possible exception of Shelley, has ever had a mind so perfectly adapted to understanding what was best and most characteristic in the philosophy of Plato, and certainly none has ever owed him a greater debt. In the case of Spenser natural disposition and circumstances combined to awaken interest in Plato.

Philosophy for the Middle Ages had been almost summed up in the name of Aristotle, and Platonism survived in a second rate form mainly through its influence on Boethius but, even thus diluted, it is plainly to be recognised in Dante and Petrarch. At the Renaissance the study of Plato became one of the chief aims of the revival of learning, and the Italian humanists, among all their services, performed none greater than that of re-introducing him to the mind of Europe. A Greek scholar from Constantinople—Gemistus Plethon—lectured on Plato, in Florence, in the year 1438.

Platonism had been strangely transformed by its passage through the Neo-Platonism of Alexandria and through the

W,   *b* superstitious Middle Ages. As taught in Florence it was from the beginning an elaborate and complex system, much more dogmatic than in Plato himself, and containing many ideas for which he provides no warrant. The lectures of Gemistus Plethon were essentially uncritical, but they ensured the spread of Platonism in Italy : Bessarion of Trebizond, Marsilio Ficino and Pico della Mirandola took up the task. Marsilio Ficino became head of the Platonist Academy at Florence; he translated Plato into Latin and wrote commentaries on him, one of which, that on the *Symposium* (" Commentarium in Convivium ") will be frequently referred to in the following pages. He also translated several of the Neo-Platonists. The teachings of Plato were intermixed and confused with the mysticism of Philo and Plotinus, and with ideas derived from the Jewish Cabala, and even from Indian and Egyptian sources. Among Spenser's own contemporaries was Giordano Bruno who owed much to the Neo-Platonists, and who certainly in various ways influenced Spenser himself. The study was taken up rapidly all over the Continent : Plato was studied not only for himself and for his own value, but his popularity became associated with the reforming movement of the day ; scholastic Catholicism had adopted Aristotle as its philosopher and had given his works an authority second only to that of the Scriptures themselves. The Reformers in setting up Platonism were founding a rival system and helping to break the chains of the old scholastic theology.

Accordingly we find the Huguenot Ramus introducing Platonism into the University of Paris and find it advancing swiftly in the German Universities. It was by no accident of association that Cambridge represented for sixteenth century England both the most ardent spirit of the Reformation and the most zealous study of Plato. When Spenser proceeded to Cambridge in 1569, the religious enthusiasm in the University was almost wholly Puritan in tone and certainly all that was intellectual in the University was Platonist ; the identification of Cambridge with Platonism lasted, in fact, for well over a century.

Spenser, keenly intellectual and deeply religious, felt fully the influence of both movements; the combined influence of Puritanism and Platonism is evident from his earliest work to his latest. They appear together in *The Shepheards Calender*, they are plain, more or less, in every part of *The Faerie Queene*, and throughout the minor poems : indeed they may be said to mutually help and illustrate each other : Spenser's Puritanism saved him from seizing upon those pagan and sensuous elements in classical literature which proved a pitfall to so many of his contemporaries; it made him blind to the more dangerous aspects of Platonism and helped to concentrate his attention on that which is noblest and most characteristic in Plato—his ethical genius; on the other hand Spenser's Platonism preserved him from the, artistically at any rate, no less dangerous pitfalls of Puritanism ; it helped to preserve him from mental narrowness by showing him the best possible examples of freedom and flexibility of mind and taught him what, as a poet, it was most essential he should know—that beauty is not only consistent with moral earnestness but may be made to contribute to it in the most powerful way. There is, as Mr Pater has remarked, "a certain asceticism amid all the varied opulence of sense, of speech and fancy natural to Plato's genius " ; it is precisely in this union of opulence, and of sense and fancy with an inward asceticism, that the resemblance to Spenser is most close.

There are, of course, certain sides of Plato's genius which have no parallel in Spenser. All those many dialogues which are concerned with definitions of general terms, with inductive reasoning, and which prepare the way for formal logic, all these of necessity offered little of which the poetic talent could lay hold. Again Spenser has no means, at least he does not contrive any means, for representing the rich variety of opinion in Plato ; Plato frequently represents in the same dialogue the most widely different opinions but without arbitrating among them ; his speakers advance views mutually inconsistent and the author declines to pronounce definitely on any one ; hence the best dialogues, though strewn with suggestive ideas, are free from dogma and give the effect of extreme flexibility of mind. This effect Spenser does not attempt to render in his poetry and, even where he follows Plato most closely, it is always with a certain difference. This imitation is nowhere closer than in the *Fowre Hymnes* where his theories of the nature of love and beauty are, in all essentials, taken from the *Phaedrus* and *Symposium*; yet he can only make his explanations consistent by sacrificing a large part of the Platonic dialogues and by buttressing up what remains with conceptions taken from the Italian Platonists; in the process the dramatic life and variety of the originals are inevitably lost; the total result, though in a sense more consistent, is less subtle, less ingenious and less profound.

We may sum up this side of the matter by saying that the subtler sides of Platonism and its complexity and variety Spenser can hardly attempt to render.

Other sides of Plato's genius were in a quite special way akin. Plato has at once a firm grip on the realities of the visible world, an intense delight in beauty of form and colour, and also a happy realisation of the unseen world which is, to him, just as vivid a reality as the material one. Like Plato, Spenser is both spiritual and sensuous, delighting in abstractions, but perceiving them so vividly that he is able to clothe and make them real. Plato also has a genius for allegory; many of the most striking passages in his works are allegories and they are nearly all of deep moral import; it is unnecessary to do more than point out how closely related this is to the essential genius of *The Faerie Queene*. Spenser has taken no actual allegory from his master but he has certainly been encouraged in his natural adherence to the form. And it may be shown that even Spenser's limitations, as regards his conception of poetry, have in some way their warrant from Plato. In the *Republic* (Bks II. and III.) Plato represents Socrates as condemning all poets who do not make instruction the direct aim of their work, who tell unedifying fables of the gods or represent heroes as acting in an unbecoming manner; Socrates even blames Homer for showing unrestrained grief in Achilles.

That Plato's was a view always to be reckoned with we can see from Sidney's *Apologie for Poetrie*, where Sidney considers at length the fact that poets were banished from the *Republic*, and shows that it applies only to such as do not aim at moral instruction ; Sidney insists upon poetic justice: the virtuous must always be rewarded, and the bad punished, otherwise there is not sufficient incentive to be good and he naïvely represents poetry as being much more excellent than history because history must sometimes show the bad prosperous and thus discourage moral behaviour. It is this view of literature and the function of poetry, founded essentially on Plato's teaching, which is worked out through the whole of *The Faerie Queene* ; the aim is entirely moral, the heroes are never permitted to do unbecoming actions without being well punished for them and poetic justice is always satisfied. It is probable that Plato would not have interpreted an ethical aim quite so narrowly but, at any rate, this is what both Sidney and Spenser thought he meant.

It might also be observed that, besides other similarities, Spenser resembles Plato in the art of narrative as such. Plato is, when he chooses, the most excellent teller of tales with infinite charm and vivacity and true dramatic power; and Spenser, in this, as in so many things, is like but on a lower scale.

Again, Plato has an intense enthusiasm for certain special virtues, such as Temperance and Justice, and has also a tendency to make them incarnate in particular persons; as Pater points out Charmides *is* Temperance, and Socrates *is* Righteousness. Here also Spenser offers the closest parallel ; his knights all incarnate some special virtue, Guyon is Temperance, Artegall is Justice, Britomart is Chastity; it is true that, though Spenser can invent types, he cannot endow them with the same vivid reality and interest, there is no figure which stands out in his pages quite like the figure of Charmides, to say nothing of Socrates. Finally, we may point out that Plato was a great lover, ardent to the utmost possible degree, yet fond also of seeking out the philosophical bases of the passion and seeking perpetually for its ethical value as an inspiration and a formative element in character.

We have only, of course, to make the comparison between them to see how immense the intellectual superiority of Plato is. Spenser cannot draw characters as real. Amid all his allegories Spenser has none at once so profoundly significant and so imaginative as the allegory of the cave in the *Republic*, or as the allegory of the winged horses and the charioteer in the *Phaedrus*. Plato's narrative of Atlantis is as romantic as any of Spenser's tales but it is much more realistic and plausible in every detail, and Spenser has nothing so daintily and unforgettably charming as the fable of the grasshoppers in the *Phaedrus*.

Still, with all these native resemblances, it is not surprising that the influence of Plato should appear almost everywhere in Spenser's work, continually recurring and repeating itself. The first two of the *Fowre Hymnes*[1] were probably written during Spenser's residence in Cambridge. Immediately after this period was composed *The Shepheards Calender*, where one eclogue at least (the October one) shows the same conception of love as in the *Hymnes*.

Throughout *The Faerie Queene* the influence of Plato is strongly manifest but especially in the first two books where it underlies the whole conception of virtue. One of the fundamental thoughts of Platonism, as explained in the *Phaedrus* and elsewhere, is that it is possible by the practice of virtue so to train and instruct the soul that it becomes conscious of wisdom and truth as visible things, and can conceive them in their native beauty as they really are. This is the state of mind which Spenser understands as Holiness and which forms the subject of the first book. It is possible that the character of Una is meant to represent the Platonic wisdom ($\sigma o\phi i a$ or $\dot{a}\rho\epsilon\tau\dot{\eta}$); throughout the many trials of the journey the face of Una is veiled from the Red Cross Knight and not until the end, when his soul is purified and his great conflict over, is she unveiled to him in her native loveliness. It is noticeable that, though the beauty of Una is great, it is not described as a physical beauty

[1] See note on p. lxxii.

but mainly by virtue of its effects. Again and again the presence of her heavenly wisdom is dwelt upon. Thus she teaches the fauns and satyrs who hang joyfully on her words and Sir Satyrane marvels at her wisdom

> "He wondred at her wisedome hevenly rare,
>   Whose like in womens witt he never knew."
>
> (I. vi. 31.)

It is she who guides the Red Cross Knight to the House of Holiness where he is to become disciplined and learn true wisdom. There are also many incidental references. One of the loveliest passages in the *Symposium* is rendered by Spenser into immortal beauty.

> "The noble hart that harbours vertuous thought,
>   And is with childe of glorious great intent,
>   Can never rest, untill it forth have brought
>   Th' eternall brood of glorie excellent."   (I. v. 1.)

One of the most interesting passages in the account of the Giant Despair (Canto ix.) is taken from Plato's *Phaedo.* In the *Phaedo* Socrates argues that, though death is better than life, it is still not permissible to commit suicide because man is, as it were, a possession of the gods and may not leave the post to which they have appointed him. So the Red Cross Knight argues in answer to Despair :

> "The terme of life is limited,
>   Ne may a man prolong, nor shorten it ;
>   The souldier may not move from watchfull sted
>   Nor leave his stand untill his Captaine bed."
>
> (I. ix. 41.)

The whole account of the contemplative life in the House of Holiness owes much to Plato. It is essentially the life of Plato's ideal man—the philosopher.

Throughout the book the conception of virtue is a Platonic one. In the *Republic* Plato shows how virtue is partly due to a good natural disposition, partly to discipline which forms habit, and partly to the good pleasure of heaven or unmerited grace. This is true of all Spenser's heroes but perhaps especially of the Red Cross Knight ; the natural disposition is excellent but, if grace for a moment leaves him, he is involved in all manner of hardships and he needs the stern discipline of the House of Holiness. Virtue, as taught by his example, does not consist in any obedience to outward rules, but is a condition of the soul, and one virtue involves practically all the others.

In the second book the correspondence is still closer. The main part of the plan, as Spenser himself states has been taken from Aristotle's *Ethics*, but the scheme is everywhere expanded and illuminated by Platonism.

In the *Timaeus*, the *Republic*, and elsewhere, Plato divides the soul into three principles : one rational and two irrational. The irrational principles are spirit or anger (θυμός) and sensuality and Temperance is the harmony resulting in the mind when the rational spirit rules. (*Republic* Bk IV.)

In the second book Guyon is the ideal of Temperance, the palmer who serves as his guide, continually helping and admonishing, represents the rational principle and, being such and nothing more, is shown in a somewhat dry and impersonal light. The first six cantos, when taken as a whole, show Guyon tempted by the first irrational principle anger and the later six cantos show him tempted by the second irrational principle— lust or passion.

In the *Laches* Plato had shown that the virtues are inseparably connected. Thus Socrates rejects, one after another, the definitions of Courage given by *Laches*, shows that courage may not only mean endurance in battle, but also the endurance of pain and reproach ; it is a certain wise strength of mind, the reasonable fortitude of a man who foresees what is coming and is very different from mere fury like that of a wild beast ; the man who has such a knowledge of good and evil as is necessary for real courage must have in addition temperance and justice and all the other virtues. This is the case with Spenser's Guyon : he is full of courage but it is reasoned and careful courage, sharply distinguished from the mere animal spirit of Pyrochles and Cymochles ; it includes fortitude as is shown by the adventures in the Cave of Mammon and Acrasia's bower and it is the inspiring spirit without which the virtue of Temperance could not exist.

The number of allusions in the second book is very large. The regality of reason is dwelt upon and the misery of the man who permits it to be ruled by his baser part.

> "Behold the ymage of mortalitie,
> And feeble nature cloth'd with fleshly tyre.
> When raging passion with fierce tyranny
> Robs reason of her dew regalitie,
> And makes it servaunt to her basest part,
> The strong it weakens with infirmitie,
> And with bold fury armes the weakest hart;
> The strong through pleasure soonest falles, the weake through
> smart."
>
> (II. i. 57.)

In the account of Guyon's visit to the Cave of Mammon and the lower world we see that Spenser cannot make even incidental reference to the hemlock without recollecting its connection with the death of Socrates.

> "Cicuta bad
> With which th' unjust Atheniens made to dy
> Wise Socrates; who, thereof quaffing glad,
> Pour'd out his life and last Philosophy
> To the fayre Critias, his dearest Belamy."
>
> (II. vii. 42.)

The essential spirit of the scene is seized though the reference is quite inaccurate, as the mention of Critias shows, and proves, as do many other quotations, that Spenser quotes from memory.

The description of the House of Temperance, in which dwells Alma or the soul, contains several passages borrowed from the *Timaeus*. At the end of the same canto the wisdom of the sages who inhabit it is compared to the wisdom of Socrates

> "whom Greece, the Nourse of all good arts,
> By Phoebus doome the wisest thought alive."
>
> (II. ix. 48.)

In the siege that is conducted against the House of Temperance by its foes, the teaching of the *Republic* is plainly present to Spenser's mind; strong affections, that is passions,

are ever struggling against the reason and aiming at bringing
the soul into captivity but there is no life so miserable as that
which is subject to their tyranny ; in the body in which Alma
or the soul reigns rightly all the parts are held in due subjection.

In the third book of *The Faerie Queene* the Platonic influence
is no less manifest. If Spenser had followed Aristotle strictly
he ought to have considered Chastity as a part of Temperance ;
if he had followed the mediaeval ideal he would have rendered
it as a strict asceticism ; but instead he is wholly Platonic.

Chastity, as exhibited in Britomart, is essentially the noble
love of the *Phaedrus*; it has nothing ascetic about it, it is
glowing and passionate, even tortured with its passion, but
it has at the same time a noble restraint, it is incapable of
baseness, it is a love inspired by and dwelling upon one image,
despising all allurements and impelled to heroic achievements.
The struggle of Chastity is against the mean and ignoble love,
as typified in the enchanter Busirane, full of sensuousness and
cruelty.

There are many direct allusions. Britomart explains to the
Red Cross Knight how all her heart is set, as according to the
Symposium, the heart of the noble lover always is, upon the
desire for honour.

> " All my delight on deedes of armes is sett,
>   To hunt out perilles and adventures hard,
>   By sea, by land, where so they may be mett,
>   Onely for honour and for high regard,
>   Without respect of richesse or reward[1]." (III. ii. 7.)

Again Spenser describes the love which is his theme almost
exactly as he describes it in the second of the *Fowre Hymnes*.

> " Most sacred fire that burnest mightily
>   In living brests, ykindled first above
>   Emongst th' eternall spheres and lamping sky,
>   And thence pour'd into men, which men call Love.
>   ......that sweete fit that doth true beautie love,
>   And chooseth vertue for his dearest Dame,
> Whence spring all noble deedes and never dying fame[2]."
> > (III. iii. 1.)

---

[1] *Hymn* I., ll. 224—231.   [2] *Ib.* ll. 63—70 and 217—224.

It is this love, Spenser explains, by which the eternal decrees of Providence are brought about. In the fifth canto Spenser makes the same contrast between the two types of love as is made by Plato in the *Symposium* and by himself in the second *Hymn*; in base minds the only effect of love is to stir up sensual desire and make them waste their time in sloth and idleness, but in noble minds it kindles the highest aspirations.

> " Ne suffereth it uncomely idlenesse
>   In his free thought to build her sluggish nest,
>   Ne suffereth it thought of ungentlenesse
>   Ever to creep into his noble brest;
>   But to the highest and the worthiest
>   Lifteth it up that els would lowly fall[1]."

(III. v. 2.)

Spenser may be said to have used up the noblest part of his ethics in the first three books of *The Faerie Queene*. In the first two he represents the Platonic conception of virtue as being essentially the health and harmony of the soul, the perfect balance of all the faculties and his first two heroes illustrate it in full.

In the third book Spenser deals with the Platonic conception of love and makes it incarnate in the person of Britomart. It is noticeable that she is never tempted as the heroes of the first two books are, all in her is perfectly noble, but at the same time there is a restlessness and fever in her which they do not possess.

In the later books Spenser, having exhausted his main Platonic inspiration, had much less assured guidance and hence, in part at any rate, the inferiority of these books in ethical value and their comparative lack of cohesion. His plan was to exhibit each virtue in turn; but he was met by the dilemma which Socrates states so eloquently in the *Laches* that each virtue seems unable to exist without the active co-operation of all the rest; thus he was almost compelled either to repeat the full portraits given in the earlier books or else, in achieving

[1] *Hymn* I., ll. 175—182.

variety, to descend to a lower level and the latter is the alternative he chooses.

In the fourth book his conception of friendship is curiously weak and unsatisfying; the noble and enthusiastic feeling which represents friendship in Plato he had already embodied in the person of Britomart, and it is significant that though Britomart is not nominally the centre of the fourth book, yet her figure continues to attract the main interest to itself.

In the Introduction Spenser shows at the outset his confusion of mind by speaking, not of the friendship which is nominally his theme, but directly of love.

> " For it of honor and all vertue is
>   The roote, and brings forth glorious floures of fame,
>   That crowne true lovers with immortal bliss,
> The meed of them that love, and do not live amisse.
>
>   Which who so list looke backe to former ages,
>   And call to count the things that then were donne,
>   Shall find that all the workes of those wise sages,
>   And brave exploits which great Heroës wonne,
>   In love were either ended or begunne:
>   Witnesse the father of Philosophie,
>   Which to his Critias, shaded oft from sunne,
>   Of love full manie lessons did apply,
> The which these Stoicke censours cannot well deny[1]."
>
> (IV. I, 2.)

The reference in the last paragraph seems to be to the *Phaedrus* but, if so, it is quoted with singular inaccuracy.

Britomart is the embodiment of noble beauty, not only physical but of the mind and soul and, wherever she appears, she inspires a feeling of awe akin to worship. In her fight with the unknown Artegall he strikes her helmet and shears a portion of it away; her face appears in such beauty that he is overwhelmed with astonishment and delight; when he raises his arm to strike her he finds himself bewitched so

---

[1] *Hymn* I., ll. 218—224 and 232—238.

that he cannot; his sword and his hand are incapable of injuring a beauty so great.

> "And he himselfe, long gazing thereupon,
> At last fell humbly down upon his knee,
> And of his wonder made religion,
> Weening some heavenly goddesse he did see,
> Or else unweeting what it else might bee;
> ......Whilest trembling horrour did his sense assayle,
> And make ech' member quake and manly heart to quayle[1]."
>
> (IV. vi. 22.)

From that moment Artegall is filled with love; but his reverence for Britomart restrains the expression of it. In the imagery of the *Phaedrus* Spenser represents his restraint as making his emotions more furious.

> "Whereby the passion grew more fierce and faine,
> Like to a stubborne steede whom strong hand would restraine."

In the eighth canto of the same book Spenser explains how one of the best characteristics of the golden age was the innocence of the love experienced during its reign but, after it passed away, love and beauty were both put to shame and beauty, which was the image of the Creator, became degraded. (IV. viii. 32.)

In the beginning of another canto Spenser weighs the advantages of family affection, love and friendship; he declares that natural affection is soon overcome by "Cupid's greater flame" but faithful friendship surpasses them both and, in this case at any rate, it is evident that Spenser means by friendship the enthusiastic rapture of Plato.

> "But faithfull friendship doth them both suppresse,
> And them with maystring discipline doth tame,
> Through thoughts aspyring to eternall fame:
> For as the soul doth rule the earthly masse,
> And all the service of the body frame,
> So love of soule doth love of bodie passe[2]."
>
> (IV. ix. 2.)

---

[1] *Hymn* I., ll. 113—119.   [2] *Hymn* II., ll. 169—182.

In the tenth canto when Scudamour describes his winning
of Amoret he tells of the gardens of Venus where there are
many pairs of friends ; he describes their affection as it is
described in the speech of Phaedrus in the *Symposium*.

> " lovers lincked in true harts consent,
> Which loved not as these for like intent,
> But on chast vertue grounded their desire
> Farre from all fraud or fayned blandishment ;
> Which, in their spirits kindling zealous fire,
> Brave thoughts and noble deedes did evermore inspire.

> Such were great Hercules and Hyllus deare
> Stout Theseus and Pirithous his feare,
> Pylades and Orestes by his side ;......
> All these, and all that ever had bene tyde
> In bands of friendship, there did live for ever,
> Whose lives although decay'd, yet loves decayed never[1]."

(IV. x. 26, 27.)

The episode of the false Florimell is an allegory embodying
Platonic thought ; Florimell is true beauty, beauty not only of
body but of mind and soul ; the false Florimell is an exact
resemblance so far as outward form is concerned but, when she
is confronted with the true beauty, she dissolves away and
becomes nothing.

In the fifth book the Platonic influence is much less than in
the preceding ones. Plato's fullest definitions of Justice are
given in the *Republic*, which is, in fact, one long argument on
the nature of Justice as revealed in the individual and in the
state. Justice in the individual consists in the harmony of the
whole nature when the reasoning principle governs and the
passions are properly subservient, while Justice in the state
consists in the proper arrangement of all its parts when every
class has its function and fulfils it. (Bk IV.)

Spenser was precluded by his scheme from accepting either
of these definitions ; the first is almost indistinguishable from

---

[1] Compare *Hymn* I., ll. 232—238.

the Temperance which he had already described in the person of Guyon; the second would have involved making Justice a social virtue and he did not mean to treat of the social virtues until he came to the second (unattempted) twelve books of *The Faerie Queene.*

The fifth book, as it stands, is a somewhat unsatisfying compromise between the two. Artegall, like the typical knight errant, goes about executing justice in the sense that he punishes evil doers and avenges wrong, but he also takes part in international affairs in the expedition to aid Belgé, etc.

Yet his fate is in some respects akin to that of the truly just man described in the *Republic*; Glaucon says that the truly just man will often be the prey of doubt and misunderstanding; he will seem to others to be different from what he is and will be assailed with all kinds of slander and evil report. So Spenser represents his Artegall on the return from his great victory as assailed by the hags Envy and Detraction.

In the sixth book Spenser's aim becomes less definitely moral; he forgets his severity of purpose and allows himself to dally at ease in the "delightful land of Faery"; there is not much Platonic influence but it occurs here and there in the love making of Calidore and Pastorella. Pastorella, in her beauty and simplicity, enchants him into contemplation:

> " So stood he still long gazing thereupon,
>   Ne any will had thence to move away.......
>   And sate there still untill the flying day
>   Was farre forth spent, discoursing diversly
>   Of sundry things as fell, to worke delay."

In Spenser's minor poems Platonic influence is shown almost entirely in his conception of love.

In the *Teares of the Muses* both Terpsichore and Erato express the same idea as that in the *Hymnes.*

> "Such high conceit of that celestiall fire,
>   The base-born brood of blindnes cannot gesse,
>   Ne ever dare their dunghill thoughts aspire
>   Unto so lottie pitch of perfectnesse[1]."

[1] See *Hymn* i., ll. 169—175.

In *Colin Clout's Come Home Againe* Spenser contrasts the love of the courtiers, which is all frivolity and folly, with the true type; the courtiers continually speak of love, "all their talk and study is of it," every man must bear the badge of some gay mistress and no man among them is esteemed " Unless, he swim in love up to the eares"; but they do not interpret love as shepherds (*i.e.* poets) interpret it; they profane his mighty mysteries and serve him in evil fashion.

The true nature of love is explained to be the underlying principle of all creation:

> " Of loves perfection perfectly to speake,
> Or of his nature rightly to define,
> Indeed (said Colin) passeth reasons reach,
> And needs his priest t' expresse his powre divine,
> For long before the world he was ybore[1],
> And bred above in Venus bosome deare :
> For by his powre the world was made of yore,
> And all that therein wondrous doth appeare.
> For how should else things so far from attone,
> And so great enemies as of them bee,
> Be ever drawne together into one
> And taught in such accordance to agree?
> Through him the cold began to covet heat,
> And water fire; the light to mount on hie
> And th' heavie downe to peize; the hungry t' eat,
> So, being former foes, they wexed friends,
> And gan by litle learne to love each other:
>
> .   .   .   .[2]
>
> But man, that had the sparke of reasons might
> More then the rest to rule his passion
> Chose for his love the fairest in his sight
> Like as himselfe was fairest by creation:
> For beautie is the bayt which with delight
> Doth man allure for to enlarge his kind;
> Beautie, the burning lamp of heavens light[3],
> Darting her beames into each feeble mynd."

---

[1] See *Hymn* I., ll. 50—56.   [2] See *Hymn* I., ll. 57—91.
[3] See *Hymn* I., ll. 106—119.

In the *Epithalamium* there is the same preference for
the inward beauty of mind and spirit over the outward beauty.
He praises in the highest terms the physical loveliness of his
bride.

> " But if ye saw that which no eyes can see,
> The inward beauty of her lively spright
> Garnisht with heavenly guifts of high degree,
> Much more then would ye wonder at that sight—
> There vertue raynes as Queene in royal throne,
> And giveth lawes alone,
> The which the base affections doe obay,
> And yeeld theyr services unto her will[1]."

Spenser's *Sonnets* again are full of the influence of Plato
and this helps to make amends for what might otherwise be a
want of interest in them ; they have not, like those of Shake-
speare and Sidney, an enthralling story to tell ; there is very
little narrative, what there is consists of only the ordinary alter-
nations of a lover's hopes and fears and many of the sonnets are
almost purely imitative and follow the usual Petrarchan con-
vention though with a style so perfect as almost to rival that of
Petrarch himself.

The greater number of his finest ideas and expressions
are suggested by Plato. The poet dwells throughout on the
exaltation of his love, its purity, the rapture and inspiration he
derives from it. He explains how it kindles light in his soul :

> " The soverayne beauty which I doo admyre,
> Witnesse the world how worthy to be prayzed !
> The light whereof hath kindled heavenly fyre
> In my fraile spirit, by her from basenesse raysed."
>
> *(Sonnet 3.)*

He goes on to explain that she has made him incapable now
of regarding anything impure, but he stands in amazement at
the sight of her celestial beauty ; astonishment arrests his pen
and makes dumb his lips. He consoles himself for her delay
by remembering that it is only the base loves which are easily

[1] See *Hymn* II., ll. 183—189.

won ; the true and noble love cannot be achieved by anything except labour and perseverance but, when once achieved, it is constant.

His beloved is full of divine fire, her beauty is heavenly, it renews the whole of nature and calms the storm of passion.

> " More then most faire, full of the living fire,
>   Kindled above unto the Maker neere ;......
>   Through your bright beams doth not the blinded guest
>   Shoot out his darts to base affections wound ;
>   But Angels come to lead fraile mindes to rest
>   In chast desires, on heavenly beauty bound,
>   You frame my thoughts and fashion me within."
>
> *(Sonnet 8.)*

He dwells on her physical perfections but repeats and emphasises the idea that her mind is fairer still.

> "But that which fairest is but few behold,
>   Her mind adornd with vertues manifold."
>
> *(Sonnet 15.)*

Her beauty allures the gaze of all but awakens reverence and represses all base desires.

> " She to her love doth lookers eyes allure;
>   And, with sterne countenance, back again doth chace
>   Their looser lookes that stir up lustes impure[1]."
>
> *(Sonnet 21.)*

His eyes are so filled with the glory of her beauty that they cannot brook the sight of anything beside; all the magnificence of the world is vain and its splendours appear as shadows.

> " Yet are mine eyes so filled with the store
>   Of that faire sight, that nothing else they brooke,
>   But·lothe the things which they did like before,
>   And can no more endure on them to looke.
>   All this world's glory seemeth vayne to me,
>   And all their showes but shadowes, saving she[2]."
>
> *(Sonnet 35.)*

---

[1] See *Hymn* II., ll. 162—168.   [2] See *Hymn* I., ll. 204—210.

She is the image of the Maker's beauty, divinely wrought and all but exciting worship.

> "The glorious image of the Maker's beautie
> My soverayne saint, the Idoll of my thought,
> Dare not henceforth, above the bounds of dewtie,
> T' accuse of pride or rashly blame for ought.
> For being, as she is, divinely wrought,......
> Such heavenly formes ought rather worship be
> Then dare be lov'd by men of meane degree."
>
> (*Sonnet* 61.)

Spenser is haunted by Plato's image of the wings of soul; he recounts how when his spirit spreads its wings it becomes clogged with mortality but the sovereign beauty of his lady resembles heaven's light and restores his soul to its true sphere.

> "Oft, when my spirit doth spred her bolder winges,
> In mind to mount up to the purest sky;
> It down is weighd with thought of earthly things,
> And clogd with burden of mortality;
> Where, when that soverayne beauty it doth spy,
> Resembling heavens glory in her light,
> Drawne with sweet pleasures bayt,. it back doth fly
> And unto heaven forgets her former flight[1]."
>
> (*Sonnet* 72.)

He returns again, and yet again, to the comparison between the inward and outward beauty, the former being the more admirable and also the image of the divine.

> "Men call you fayre, and you doe credit it,
> For that your selfe ye dayly such doe see:
> But the true fayre, that is the gentle wit
> And vertuous mind, is much more praysed of me
> ......that is true beautie: that doth argue you
> To be divine, and borne of heavenly seed;
> Deriv'd from that fayre Spirit, from whom al true
> And perfect beauty did at first proceed[2]."
>
> (*Sonnet* 79.)

[1] See *Hymn* I., ll. 168—182.   [2] See *Hymn* II., ll. 112—119.

He sees nothing but the image of the heavenly ray as revealed in her, the true idea and type of beauty in itself, in contemplation of her he supports and sustains his soul.

> "Ne ought I see, though in the clearest day,
> When others gaze upon theyr shadowes vaine,
> But th' only image of that heavenly ray
> Whereof some glance doth in mine eie remayne.
> Of which beholding the Idaea playne,
> Through contemplation of my purest part,
> With light thereof I doe my selfe sustayne,
> And thereon feed my love-affamisht hart[1]."

(Sonnet 87.)

II.

THE INFLUENCE OF PLATO ON THE "FOWRE HYMNES."

As will have been perceived from the foregoing brief survey the influence of Plato on Spenser is a very profound one. It provides him with a continual inspiration and moulds the whole of his general conception of virtue as well as a lofty theory of love. It is in this theory of love that the influence of Plato is most immediately and persistently shown, and the theory itself is expressed most clearly and definitely in the *Fowre Hymnes*. They were not published until the year 1596, but, as Spenser himself explains in the Introduction, two of them had been written much earlier. The *Hymnes* of Love and Beauty "too much pleased those of like age and disposition," and, since the number of copies distributed made it impossible for the poet to call them in, he determined to amend them and, "by way of retractation, to reforme them, making, in stead of those two *Hymnes* of earthly or naturall love and beautie, two others of heavenly and celestiall."

So in the *Hymne of Heavenly Love* Spenser laments

> "Many lewd layes (ah! woe is me the more!)
> In praise of that mad fit which fooles call love,
> I have in th' heat of youth made heretofore."

[1] See *Hymn* II., ll. 210—235.

The accusation of lewdness certainly could not be brought against the first two hymns as they stand, but it is possible that Spenser altered them or else that he is referring to other love poetry.

The theory of love and beauty expressed in all four is taken mainly from the erotic dialogues of Plato—the *Phaedrus* and *Symposium*. Spenser harmonises the different views expressed in them as far as he can, and omits what he has no place for though occasionally, it must be admitted, he is led into inconsistencies.

The speech of Socrates in the *Phaedrus* is one clear and consistent whole, but the speakers in the *Symposium* express different points of view which are not in all respects easy to reconcile; Spenser takes something from almost every one, blending and harmonising in his own way. He also borrows freely from the Italian Platonists, at times to explain Plato, sometimes to amplify and occasionally to introduce totally fresh matter; he relies on them most in the two later hymns—those on Heavenly Love and Heavenly Beauty—where Plato, naturally, could supply less of a model.

The student will probably find that the simplest way of studying the *Hymnes* is to take first those portions which are due to the direct influence of Plato and then consider those which may be traced to the Italian Platonists.

In the *Phaedrus* love is explained in its relation to beauty and as being essentially the excitement produced by the sight of beauty; this explanation involves reference to two of Plato's favourite doctrines—that of recollection and that of ideas.

The doctrine of recollection is developed most fully in the *Meno*: the soul of man has undergone many incarnations; it is always passing from one body to another, in its different stages of existence, and especially in the upper world, it has seen and learnt all things but, when it comes upon earth, the body obscures and darkens it, and it forgets the greater part of its knowledge. It is capable, however, of recollecting all that it has known and it does so mainly by association; when it clearly knows or perceives one thing then it is reminded of many others. Socrates proves his point by the case of the slave who is led to demonstrate a difficult problem in geometry.

In the *Parmenides* Plato developes the doctrine of ideas : all objects of sense are fleeting and changeable but everything that we can see has its eternal idea or prototype ; thus, removed from the material world of birth and death and change, there is another world of pure and perfect forms, imperceptible to the earthly senses, and which, for dwellers in this world, can be apprehended by reason alone ; each single form is in itself pure and unchangeable and eternal ; each one answers to some visible object and all visible objects are what they are, possessed of form and qualities, only because they share in the divine essence of their corresponding ideas.

In the *Phaedrus* Socrates begins his praise of love by saying that, like the gift of prophecy and the gift of poetic song, it is a divine madness.

The soul is immortal ; when fully winged it soars upward and is the ruler of the universe but the imperfect soul loses its feathers and, settling on the ground, receives an earthly frame. The wing is intended to soar aloft and carry the soul to the upper region where the gods dwell. Beauty, wisdom and goodness are all divine things and nourish the wing of the soul : τὸ δὲ θεῖον καλόν, σοφόν, ἀγαθόν, καὶ πᾶν ὅτι τοιοῦτον· τούτοις δὴ τρέφεταί τε καὶ αὔξεται μάλιστά γε τὸ τῆς ψυχῆς πτέρωμα[1].

When fed upon evil, foulness and the like the wing wastes away : αἰσχρῷ δὲ καὶ κακῷ καὶ τοῖς ἐναντίοις φθίνει τε καὶ διόλλυται.

Those souls which have sufficient strength can follow the gods and enter the heaven of heavens ; reaching this the divine intelligence rejoices to behold reality, it gazes upon truth and is inspired and made happy by the sight : in its course it beholds justice and temperance and true knowledge, not in the form of created things but as they really are. καθορᾷ μὲν αὐτὴν δικαιοσύνην, καθορᾷ δὲ σωφροσύνην, καθορᾷ δὲ ἐπιστήμην[2].

---

[1] *Phaedrus* 246.
[2] *Ib.* 247. See also notes pp. 54, 69.

Many souls, however, are unable to sustain their flight, their wings are broken, they descend to earth and become embodied in human forms[1]. The more they have seen of truth in the upper world the more excellent are their natures upon earth. ἀλλὰ τὴν μὲν πλεῖστα ἰδοῦσαν εἰς γονὴν ἀνδρὸς γενησομένου φιλοσόφου ἢ φιλοκάλου ἢ μουσικοῦ τινὸς καὶ ἐρωτικοῦ.

The man who beholds beauty here upon earth is transported by it, not for its own sake only but because it reminds him of the beauty, lofty, divine, and imperishable, which he has seen in the world above. Not all men are equally delighted, for there is a great difference in the power of recollection; some souls do not easily recall the things of the other world "they may have[2] seen them for a short time only, or have been unfortunate in their earthly lot, and may have lost the memory of the holy things which they once perceived through some evil and corrupting association." Few only retain an adequate remembrance of them; and they, when they behold any image of that other world, are rapt in amazement; but they are ignorant of what this rapture means, because they do not clearly perceive. For there is no light in the earthly copies of justice or temperance or any of the higher qualities which are precious to souls; they are seen through a glass dimly; and there are few who, going to the images, behold in them the realities, and they only with difficulty. They might have seen beauty shining in brightness, when, with the happy band following in the train of Zeus, as we philosophers, or of other gods as others did, they saw a vision and were initiated into mysteries which may be truly called most blessed, and which we celebrated in our state of innocence; having no experience of evils as yet to come; admitted to the sight of apparitions innocent and simple and calm and happy, shining in company with the celestial forms; and coming to earth we find her here too, shining in clearness through the clearest aperture of sense. For sight is the keenest of our bodily senses; though not by

[1] *Phaedrus* 248.

[2] Jowett's translation. For parallel passages in the original see notes pp. 69, 71. *Phaedrus* 250.

that is wisdom seen ; her loveliness would have been trans-
porting if there had been a visible image of her, and the same
is true of the loveliness of the other ideas as well. But this is
the privilege of beauty, that she is the loveliest and also the most
palpable to sight[1]. Now he who is not newly initiated or who
has become corrupted, does not easily rise out of this world
to the sight of true beauty in the other ; he looks only at her
earthly namesake, and instead of being awed at the sight of
her, like a brutish beast he rushes on to enjoy and beget ; he
consorts with wantonness and is not afraid or ashamed of
pursuing pleasure in violation of nature. But he whose initia-
tion is recent, and who has been the spectator of many glories
in the other world, is amazed when he sees anyone having a
godlike face or form, which is the expression of divine beauty ;
and at first a shudder runs through him and again the old awe
steals over him ; then looking upon the face of his beloved as
of a god, he reverences him, and if he were not afraid of being
thought a downright madman, he would sacrifice to his beloved
as to the image of a god ; then as he gazes on him there is
a sort of reaction, and the shudder naturally passes into an
unusual heat and perspiration ; for as he receives the effluence
of beauty through the eyes, the wing moistens and he warms.
And as he warms, the parts out of which the wing grew, and
which had been hitherto closed and rigid, and had prevented
the wing from shooting forth, are melted, and as nourishment
streams upon him, the lower end of the wing begins to swell
and grow from the root upwards ; and the growth extends
under the whole soul for once the whole was winged[2]."

Socrates proceeds to explain that, when the lover is separated
from the beloved, the growth of the wing is arrested and the
whole soul is in a state of irritation and pain but is still
delighted at the recollection of the beauty it has beheld

"And from both of them together the soul is oppressed at
the strangeness of her condition, and is in a great strait and
excitement, and in her madness can neither sleep by night
nor abide in her place by day[3]. And wherever she thinks that

[1] See note p. 47.   [2] *Phaedrus* 250, 251.   [3] See note p. 48.

she will behold the beautiful one, thither in her desire she runs.
And when she has seen him, and bathed herself with the waters
of desire, her constraint is loosened, and she is refreshed and
has no more pangs and pains ; and this is the sweetest of all
pleasures at the time, and is the reason why the soul of the
lover will never forsake his beautiful one, whom he esteems
above all ; he has forgotten mother and brethren and com-
panions, and he thinks nothing of the neglect and loss of
his property[1].

In the most famous of all similes Socrates compares the
soul to a figure of a composite nature—a pair of winged horses
and a charioteer. The charioteer is noble but the horses are
mixed ; one of them is good and the other is bad : the noble
horse is a lover of honour and modesty and temperance and
a follower of true glory ; he does not need the whip but can
be guided by admonition only: the dark horse will obey
nothing but the whip and spur, and even those with difficulty[2].

" Now when the charioteer beholds the vision of love, and
has his whole soul warmed through sense, and is full of the
prickings and ticklings of desire, the obedient steed, then as
always under the government of shame, refrains from leaping
on the beloved ; but the other, without heeding the blows of
the whip, plunges and runs away[3]."

ὅταν δ' οὖν ὁ ἡνίοχος ἰδὼν τὸ ἐρωτικὸν ὄμμα, πᾶσαν αἰσθήσει
διαθερμήνας τὴν ψυχήν, γαργαλισμοῦ τε καὶ πόθου κέντρων ὑπο-
πλησθῇ, ὁ μὲν εὐπειθὴς τῷ ἡνιόχῳ τῶν ἵππων, ἀεί τε καὶ τότε
αἰδοῖ βιαζόμενος, ἑαυτὸν κατέχει μὴ ἐπιπηδᾶν τῷ ἐρωμένῳ.

The charioteer and the noble steed indignantly oppose him
but his violence urges them on. "And now they are at the
spot and behold the flashing beauty of the beloved ; which
when the charioteer sees, his memory is carried to the true
beauty whom he beholds in company with Modesty set in
her holy place. He sees her but he is afraid and falls back-
ward in adoration."

[1] *Phaedrus* 251, 252.   [2] *Ib.* 247, 253.
[3] *Ib.* 254.

καὶ πρὸς αὐτῷ τ᾽ ἐγένοντο καὶ εἶδον τὴν ὄψιν τὴν τῶν παιδικῶν
ἀστράπτουσαν · ἰδόντος δὲ τοῦ ἡνιόχου ἡ μνήμη πρὸς τὴν τοῦ κάλλους
φύσιν ἠνέχθη, καὶ πάλιν εἶδεν αὐτὴν μετὰ σωφροσύνης ἐν ἁγνῷ
βάθρῳ βεβῶσαν[1].

The struggle is often repeated. "And when this has
happened several times and the villain has ceased from his
wanton way, he is tamed and humbled, and follows the will
of the charioteer, and when he sees the beautiful one he is
ready to die of fear. And from that time forward the soul
of the lover follows the beloved in modesty and holy fear."

ὅταν δὲ ταὐτὸν πολλάκις πάσχων ὁ πονηρὸς τῆς ὕβρεως λήξῃ,
ταπεινωθεὶς ἕπεται ἤδη τῇ τοῦ ἡνιόχου προνοίᾳ, καὶ ὅταν ἴδῃ τὸν
καλόν, φόβῳ διόλλυται · ὥστε συμβαίνει τότ᾽ ἤδη τὴν τοῦ ἐραστοῦ
ψυχὴν τοῖς παιδικοῖς αἰδουμένην τε καὶ δεδιυίαν ἔπεσθαι[2].

According to Socrates in the *Phaedrus*, then, love is
essentially the excitement and rapture produced by the sight
of beauty, and beauty is able to move so powerfully because
it is of all earthly things that which possesses the closest
resemblance to its heavenly idea or prototype or, rather,
appears to possess the closest resemblance since it appeals
to the clearest of the senses; the sight of it arouses the
reminiscence of the divine beauty, and of the other ideas as
well, and of the eternal world in which all were seen. The
Phaedrus explains the excitement produced by love as being
essentially a state of inspiration or divine madness; the soul
which was once winged becomes winged again and capable
of soaring to the exalted world which it formerly inhabited.
Further, the *Phaedrus* carefully distinguishes between that
excitement of love which is sensuous and has no reverence,
and that excitement which is mainly spiritual and is full of
modesty and awe; the two are sharply contrasted, but it is
noticeable that they are both described as possible to one and
the same person. It is the same individual who is capable of
feeling each, and not only that, but there is the fiercest struggle
between the two, owing to the contending principles in the lover

---

[1] *Phaedrus* 254.   [2] *Ib.* 254.

himself; when the ignoble element prevails the love is sensuous
and unrestrained but, when the noble element conquers, then
it is wholly pure. This pure love is a discipline for the whole
mind and nature, those who experience it pass their lives in
happiness and harmony: "when the end comes, they are light
and ready to fly away...nor can human discipline or divine
inspiration confer any greater blessing on man than this[1]."

The leading ideas of the *Phaedrus* are expressed, more or
less, in all of the *Fowre Hymnes*. Thus in the *Hymne in Honour
of Love* the heavenly character of beauty is dwelt upon.

> "Therefore in choice of love he doth desyre
> That seemes on earth most heavenly to embrace,
> That same is Beautie, borne of heavenly race.
>
> For sure of all that in this mortall frame
> Contained is, nought more divine doth seeme,
> Or that resembleth more th' immortall flame
> Of heavenly light, then Beauties glorious beame.
> What wonder then, if with such rage extreme
> Fraile men, whose eyes seek heavenly things to see,
> At sight thereof so much enravisht bee?" (ll. 110—119.)

Their distress is described:

> "Thenceforth they playne, and make ful piteous mone
> Unto the author of their balefull bane:
> The daies they waste, the nights they grieve and grone,
> Their lives they loath, and heavens light disdaine;
> No light but that, whose lampe doth yet remaine
> Fresh burning in the image of their eye,
>
> They deigne to see, and seeing it still dye."
>
> (ll. 127—133.)

The inspiration of love is described by Plato's image of the
wings:

> "For love is Lord of truth and loialtie,
> Lifting himselfe out of the lowly dust
> On golden plumes up to the purest skie,
> Above the reach of loathly sinfull lust,
> Whose base affect through cowardly distrust
> Of his weake wings dare not to heaven fly,
> But like a moldwarpe in the earth doth ly."
>
> (ll. 176—182.)

---

[1] *Phaedrus* 256. See also notes p. 52.

" Such is the powre of that sweet passion
  That it all sordid basenesse doth expell,
  And the refyned mind doth newly fashion
  Unto a fairer forme, which now doth dwell
  In his high thought, that would it selfe excell,
  Which he beholding still with constant sight
  Admires the mirrour of so heavenly light.

  Whose image printing in his deepest wit,
  He thereon feeds his hungrie fantasy,
  Still full, yet never satisfyde with it;
  Like Tantale, that in store doth sterved ly,
  So doth he pine in most satiety;
  For nought may quench his infinite desyre,
  Once kindled through that first conceived fyre.

  Thereon his mynd affixed wholly is,
  Ne thinks on ought but how it to attaine;
  His care, his joy, his hope is all on this,
  That seemes in it all blisses to containe,
  In sight whereof all other blisse seemes vaine:
  Thrise happie man ! might he the same possesse,
  He faines himselfe, and doth his fortune blesse.

  And though he do not win his wish to end,
  Yet thus farre happie he himselfe doth weene,
  That heavens such happie grace did to him lend,
  As thing on earth so heavenly to have seene......
  Whose sole aspect he counts felicitye. " (ll. 190—217.)

In the *Hymne in Honour of Beautie* Spenser speaks of
the pattern or idea of beauty, in itself beyond the apprehension
of mortal sense, but according to which all beautiful things are
fashioned :

"That wondrous Paterne, wheresoere it bee,......
  Is perfect Beautie, which all men adore ;
  Whose face and feature doth so much excell
  All mortall sence, that none the same may tell.

  Thereof as every earthly thing partakes
  Or more or lesse, by influence divine,
  So it more faire accordingly it makes,
  And the grosse matter of this earthly myne
  Which clotheth it thereafter doth refyne,
  Doing away the drosse which dims the light
  Of that faire beame which therein is empight." (ll. 36—49.)

> " That is the thing which giveth pleasant grace
> To all things faire, that kindleth lively fyre,
> Light of thy lampe ; which, shyning in the face,
> Thence to the soule darts amorous desyre,
> And robs the harts of those which it admyre."
>
> (ll. 57—61.)

Beauty is often abused but is none the less excellent in herself :

> " And oft it falles, (aye me, the more to rew !)
> That goodly beautie, albe heavenly borne,
> Is foule abusd, and that celestiall hew,
> Which doth the world with her delight adorne,
> Made but the bait of sinne and sinners scorne......"
>
> (ll. 148—152.)

> " Yet nathëmore is that faire beauties blame,
> But theirs that do abuse it unto ill."
>
> (ll. 155—156.)

> " But ye, faire Dames ! the worlds deare ornaments
> And lively images of heavens light,
> Let not your beames with such disparagements
> Be dimd, and your bright glorie darkned quight ;
> But, mindfull still of your first countries sight,
> Doe still preserve your first informed grace,
> Whose shadow yet shynes in your beauteous face."
>
> (ll. 162—168.)

Spenser draws as emphatic a contrast between love and lust as Plato does between the lover and the not-lover, and he praises in equally zealous terms that love which is loyal and patient.

Socrates had compared the lover to the mirror in which the beloved is beholding himself, though he is not aware of it, and so with Spenser :

> " Loath that foule blot, that hellish fiërbrand,
> Disloiall lust faire beauties foulest blame,
> That base affections, which your eares would bland
> Commend to you by loves abused name,
> But is indeede the bondslave of defame ;......
> But gentle Love, that loiall is and trew,
> Will more illumine your resplendent ray,

> And adde more brightnesse to your goodly hew,
> From light of his pure fire; which, by like way
> Kindled of yours, your likenesse doth display;
> Like as two mirrours, by opposd reflexion,
> Doe both expresse the faces first impression."
>
> (ll. 169—182.)

In the *Hymne of Heavenly Love* Spenser finds it easy enough to use Plato's imagery for dealing with an emotion that is not concerned with any human being, but is spiritual in its very essence. He begins by praising the exaltation of such a love:

> " Love, lift me up upon thy golden wings,
> From this base world unto thy heavens hight,
> Where I may see those admirable things
> Which there thou workest by thy soveraine might,
> Farre above feeble reach of earthly sight."
>
> (ll. 1—5.)

Thus Spenser imagines himself about to describe a beauty he has already beheld, though whether, like the souls in Plato, he has beheld it before entering upon this life or whether, like Dante, he has seen it in the flesh, he does not explain; at any rate it is this beauty which he has already beheld that he wishes to describe to men, and does so in the *Hymne of Heavenly Beautie*:

> " Rapt with the rage of mine own ravisht thought,
> Through contemplation of those goodly sights,
> And glorious images in heaven wrought,
> Whose wondrous beauty, breathing sweet delights
> Do kindle love in high conceipted sprights;
> I faine to tell the things that I behold,
> But feele my wits to faile, and tongue to fold.
>
> Vouchsafe then, O thou most Almightie Spright!
> From whom all guifts of wit and knowledge flow,
> To shed into my breast some sparkling light
> Of thine eternall Truth, that I may show
> Some litle beames to mortall eyes below
> Of that immortall beautie, there with thee,
> Which in my weake distraughted mynd I see;

> That with the glorie of so goodly sight
> The hearts of men, which fondly here admyre
> Faire seeming shewes, and feed on vaine delight,
> Transported with celestiall desyre
> Of those faire formes, may lift themselves up hyer,
> And learne to love, with zealous humble dewty,
> Th' eternall fountaine of that heavenly beauty."

(ll. 1—21.)

Spenser, it should be noted, considers the 'ideas' of Plato as being inherent in the Godhead. Plato speaks of the ideas of temperance, justice, wisdom and the rest which have no representatives on earth other than the most feeble copies; so Spenser argues from the beauty of what can be seen to the much greater and more wonderful beauty of the "essential parts" of God, and from them again to the still more surpassing loveliness of the divine nature itself.

> " Cease then, my tongue! and lend unto my mynd
> Leave to bethinke how great that beautie is,
> Whose utmost parts so beautifull I fynd;
> How much more those essentiall parts of his,
> His truth, his love, his wisedome, and his blis,
> His grace, his doome, his mercy, and his might,
> By which he lends us of himselfe a sight ! "

(ll. 106—112.)

The earthly images, Plato says, have no light in them compared with the reality; so the earthly manifestation of God is weak and poor compared to the divine light:

> " Those unto all he daily doth display,
> And shew himselfe in th' image of his grace,
> As in a looking-glasse, through which he may
> Be seene of all his creatures vile and base,
> That are unable else to see his face,
> His glorious face! which glistereth else so bright,
> That th' Angels selves can not endure his sight."

(ll. 113—119.)

Imperfect, however, as the resemblances of God upon earth are, they are all that is possible to man, and by the sight of earth's beauty the mind can be inspired and exalted above itself and then achieves truly the vision of the divine:

"The meanes, therefore, which unto us is lent
Him to behold, is on his workes to looke,
Which he hath made in beauty excellent,
And in the same, as in a brasen booke
To reade enregistred in every nooke
His goodnesse, which his beautie doth declare;
For all thats good is beautifull and faire.

Thence gathering plumes of perfect speculation,
To impe the wings of thy high flying mynd,
Mount up aloft through heavenly contemplation,
From this darke world, whose damps the soule do blynd,
And, like the native brood of Eagles kynd,
On that bright Sunne of Glorie fixe thine eyes,
Clear'd from grosse mists of fraile infirmities."

(ll. 127—140.)

Socrates says, in the *Phaedrus*, that wisdom is the loveliest
of all the ideas and that her beauty would have been trans-
porting if there had been any visible image of her. Spenser
imagines her as made visible in the heaven of heavens:

"There in his bosome Sapience doth sit,
The soveraine dearling of the Deity,
Clad like a Queene in royall robes, most fit
For so great powre and peerelesse majesty,
And all with gemmes and jewels gorgeously
Adornd, that brighter than the starres appeare,
And make her native brightnes seem more cleare."

(ll. 183—189.)

Spenser, like many other poets, loves the gorgeous Catholic
imagery even while he rejects its dogma ; it is curious to notice
how he contrives to employ this imagery to clothe the abstrac-
tions of his Platonism; thus in this hymn he turns Sapience
into a kind of Virgin Mary, crowned with gold and carrying a
sceptre with which she sways the whole heaven and earth. Her
beauty, inasmuch as she is Wisdom, is far beyond that of all
other things:

"The fairenesse of her face no tongue can tell;
For she the daughters of all wemens race,
And Angels eke, in beautie doth excell,

> Sparkled on her from Gods owne glorious face,
> And more increast by her owne goodly grace,
> That it doth farre exceed all humane thought,
> Ne can on earth compared be to ought."
>
> (ll. 204—210.)

This Wisdom is the source of perfect happiness and transforms the human being wholly into the spirit :

> " But who so may, thrise happie man him hold,
> Of all on earth whom God so much doth grace,
> And lets his owne Beloved to behold ;
> For in the view of her celestiall face
> All joy, all blisse, all happinesse, have place ;
> Ne ought on earth can want unto the wight
> Who of her selfe can win the wishfull sight."
>
> (ll. 239—245.)

> " None thereof worthy be, but those whom shee
> Vouchsafeth to her presence to receave,
> And letteth them her lovely face to see,
> Whereof such wondrous pleasures they conceave,
> And sweet contentment, that it doth bereave
> Their soule of sense, through infinite delight,
> And them transport from flesh into the spright."
>
> (ll. 253—259.)

In the *Symposium* various views of love are given according to the personality of the speakers.

Phaedrus, who is the first, begins by affirming that Love is the eldest of the gods and there is no record of his parents ; he quotes Hesiod to the effect that first of all there was chaos and then the earth and love, but love was the first of all the gods[1].

So in the *Hymne in Honour of Love* Spenser represents the birth of love :

> " For ere this worlds still moving mighte masse,
> Out of great Chaos ugly prison crept,
> In which his goodly face long hidden was
> From heavens view, and in deepe darknesse kept,

---

[1] *Symposium* 178. See also notes p. 45.

W. *d*

> Love, that had now long time securely slept
> In Venus lap, unarmed then and naked,
> Gan reare his head, by Clotho being waked."
>
> (ll. 57—63.)

Phaedrus goes on to explain that love is not only the eldest
of the gods, he is the source of the greatest benefits. The lover
and the beloved encourage each other in the practice of virtue :
" For the principle which ought to be the guide of men who
would nobly live—that principle, I say, neither kindred nor
honour nor wealth nor any other motive is able to implant
so well as love. Of what am I speaking? Of the sense of
honour and dishonour without which neither states nor indi-
viduals ever do any good or great work....If there were only
some way of contriving that a state or an army should be
made up of lovers and their loves, they would be the very best
governors of their own city...and when fighting at one another's
side they would overcome the world. For what lover would
not choose rather to be seen by all mankind than by his beloved
either when abandoning his post or throwing away his arms?
He would be ready to die a thousand deaths rather than to
endure this....The veriest coward would become an inspired
hero, equal to the bravest, at such a time. Love would inspire
him....Love will make men dare to die for their beloved—love
alone ; and women as well as men."

πρεσβύτατος δὲ ὢν μεγίστων ἀγαθῶν ἡμῖν αἴτιός ἐστιν....ὃ γὰρ
χρὴ ἀνθρώποις ἡγεῖσθαι παντὸς τοῦ βίου τοῖς μέλλουσι καλῶς
βιώσεσθαι, τοῦτο οὔτε συγγένεια οἷά τε ἐμποιεῖν οὕτω καλῶς οὔτε
τιμαὶ οὔτε πλοῦτος οὔτ' ἄλλο οὐδὲν ὡς ἔρως. λέγω δὲ δὴ τί τοῦτο;
τὴν ἐπὶ μὲν τοῖς αἰσχροῖς αἰσχύνην, ἐπὶ δὲ τοῖς καλοῖς φιλοτιμίαν·
οὐ γὰρ ἔστιν ἄνευ τούτων οὔτε πόλιν οὔτε ἰδιώτην μεγάλα καὶ καλὰ
ἔργα ἐξεργάζεσθαι...εἰ οὖν μηχανή τις γένοιτο ὥστε πόλιν γενέσθαι
ἢ στρατόπεδον ἐραστῶν τε καὶ παιδικῶν, οὐκ ἔστιν ὅπως ἂν
ἄμεινον οἰκήσειαν τὴν ἑαυτῶν ἢ ἀπεχόμενοι πάντων τῶν αἰσχρῶν
καὶ φιλοτιμούμενοι πρὸς ἀλλήλους, καὶ μαχόμενοί γ' ἂν μετ' ἀλλήλων
οἱ τοιοῦτοι νικῷεν ἂν ὀλίγοι ὄντες ὡς ἔπος εἰπεῖν πάντας ἀνθρώπους·
ἐρῶν γὰρ ἀνὴρ ὑπὸ παιδικῶν ὀφθῆναι ἢ λιπὼν τάξιν ἢ ὅπλα ἀποβα-
λὼν ἧττον ἂν δή που δέξαιτο ἢ ὑπὸ πάντων τῶν ἄλλων, καὶ πρὸ

τούτου τεθνάναι ἂν πολλάκις ἔλοιτο·...οὐδεὶς οὕτω κακὸς ὅντινα οὐκ
ἂν αὐτὸς ὁ Ἔρως ἔνθεον ποιήσειε πρὸς ἀρετήν, ὥστε ὅμοιον εἶναι τῷ
ἀρίστῳ φύσει·...καὶ μὴν ὑπεραποθνήσκειν γε μόνοι ἐθέλουσιν οἱ
ἐρῶντες, οὐ μόνον ὅτι ἄνδρες, ἀλλὰ καὶ αἱ γυναῖκες[1].

Phaedrus quotes the examples of Alkestis, Orpheus and
Achilles as a proof of what the power of love will effect. He
concludes by saying : " Love is the eldest and noblest and
mightiest of the gods and the chiefest author and giver of
virtue in life and happiness after death."

οὕτω δὴ ἔγωγέ φημι Ἔρωτα θεῶν καὶ πρεσβύτατον καὶ τιμιώτα-
τον καὶ κυριώτατον εἶναι εἰς ἀρετῆς καὶ εὐδαιμονίας κτῆσιν ἀνθρώποις
καὶ ζῶσι καὶ τελευτήσασιν[2].

So in the *Hymne in Honour of Love* Spenser describes the
wonderful tasks men will perform for the sake of love :

"Then forth he casts in his unquiet thought,
  What he may do, her favour to obtaine ;
  What brave exploit, what perill hardly wrought
  What puissant conquest, what adventurous paine,
  May please her best, and grace unto him gaine ;
  He dreads no danger, nor misfortune feares,
  His faith, his fortune, in his breast he beares.

Thou art his god, thou art his mightie guyde,
  Thou, being blind, letst him not see his feares,
  But cariest him to that which he hath eyde,
  Through seas, through flames, through thousand swords and speares ;
  Ne ought so strong that may his force withstand,
  With which thou armest his resistlesse hand."

(ll. 218—230.)

Like Phaedrus, Spenser quotes the examples of Achilles and
Orpheus :

" Witnesse Leander in the Euxine waves,
  And stout Æneas in the Trojane fyre,
  Achilles preassing through the Phrygian glaives,
  And Orpheus, daring to provoke the yre
  Of damned fiends, to get his love retyre ;
  For both through heaven and hell thou makest way
  To win them worship which to thee obay.

[1] *Symposium* 178, 179.   [2] *Ib.* 180.

> And if, by all these perils and these paynes,
> He may but purchase lyking in her eye,
> What heavens of joy then to himselfe he faynes!
> Eftsoones he wypes quite out of memory
> Whatever ill before he did aby :
> Had it bene death, yet would he die againe,
> To live thus happie as her grace to gaine."
>
> (ll. 231—244.)

The speech of Phaedrus has dwelt mainly upon the inspiration of love and the heroic deeds which it impels the lover to achieve.

The speech of Pausanias treats of the difference between the vulgar lover, who loves the body only, and has no care for the soul, whose love is inconstant, and the love of the noble mind which is unchanging :

"Evil is the vulgar lover who loves the body rather than the soul, and who is inconstant because he is a lover of the inconstant, and therefore when the bloom of youth which he was desiring is over, takes wing and flies away in spite of all his words and promises ; whereas the love of the noble mind which is one with the unchanging is lifelong."

πονηρὸς δ' ἐστὶν ἐκεῖνος ὁ ἐραστὴς ὁ πάνδημος, ὁ τοῦ σώματος μᾶλλον ἢ τῆς ψυχῆς ἐρῶν· καὶ γὰρ οὐδὲ μόνιμός ἐστιν, ἅτε οὐδὲ μονίμου ἐρῶν πράγματος. ἅμα γὰρ τῷ τοῦ σώματος ἄνθει λήγοντι, οὗπερ ἤρα, "οἴχεται ἀποπτάμενος," πολλοὺς λόγους καὶ ὑποσχέσεις καταισχύνας· ὁ δὲ τοῦ ἤθους χρηστοῦ ὄντος ἐραστὴς διὰ βίου μένει, ἅτε μονίμῳ συντακείς[1].

"And this is the reason why a hasty attachment is held to be dishonourable because time is the true test of this as of most other things."

In the *Hymne in Honour of Love* Spenser makes this same contrast between the base love which is a love of the body only, soon coming and going, and the noble love which is a love of the mind and therefore steadfast :

> "So hard those heavenly beauties be enfyred
> As things divine, least passions doe impresse,

[1] *Symposium* 183.

The more of steadfast mynds to be admyred,
The more they stayed be on stedfastnesse ;
But baseborne mynds such lamps regard the lesse,
Which at first blowing take not hastie fyre ;
Such fancies feele no love, but loose desyre.

(ll. 169—175.)

Pausanias, it might be remarked, carefully points out the genealogy of the two loves ; one is derived from the heavenly Aphrodite, the daughter of Uranus (Aphrodite Urania), and the other is the daughter of Zeus and Dione (Aphrodite Pandemos), and the two kinds of love correspond to the two goddesses, the one being heavenly and exalted and the other base and common. Spenser says nothing of the genealogy but he is careful to preserve the contrast.

Eryximachus is the physician of the party and he approaches the phenomenon of love from a totally different point of view ; he does not consider it, as Phaedrus does, entirely from the side of inspiration, nor does he, like Pausanias, dwell on the contrast between the two kinds as essentially a moral contrast. His speech is as that of a scientific man naturally would be ; instead of beginning by praising love he attempts to explain it and treats it from a purely impersonal standpoint.

He agrees with Pausanias that there are two kinds of love, he calls one healthy and one diseased, but finds the same double kind of love in animals and plants as well as in man. All the art of medicine consists in knowing the loves and desires of the body; the good physician is he who is able to turn the bad loves into good ones, and who can reconcile hostile elements. The most hostile are the most opposite, such as hot and cold, moist and dry and the like. These principles exist not only in the body, but in all nature, and the course of the seasons is full of them : " When, as I was saying, the elements of hot and cold, moist and dry, attain the harmonious love of one another, and blend in temperance and harmony, they bring to men, animals and vegetables, health and plenty ! "

This idea is not used by Spenser, at any rate not directly, but, as will be seen later, it is interpreted in a much more elaborate way by Ficino, who explains that love is the concord binding all the elements together, and it is this elaborated form which Spenser employs [1].

The speech of Aristophanes is mostly meant as comedy though it has, underlying the comedy, a serious meaning. He explains that men were originally created double; they were round, having two faces on a round neck, four hands and four feet and the rest to correspond. Their strength and insolence were so great that they attempted to scale heaven and attack the gods. The gods were divided between the determination to quell their pride and the fear of losing sacrifices if they destroyed them. In this extremity Zeus hit on an expedient; he cut them in two and made them as they now are. Ever since the two halves have gone about the world, searching for each other, and when they find each other they are overwhelmed with delight.

"And when one of them finds his other half...the pair are lost in an amazement of love and friendship and intimacy, and one will not be out of the other's sight, as I may say, even for a moment: they will pass their whole lives together; yet they could not explain what they desire of one another....And the reason is that human nature was originally one and we were a whole, and the desire and pursuit of the whole is called love [2]."

This conception was too grotesque to be used by Spenser in its entirety and he prefers to accept Ficino's explanation of the harmony existing between lovers, which is, that they are born under the ascendency of the same stars or corresponding signs, and therefore, by stellar influence, their inner or aethereal bodies are made to correspond [3].

Spenser, however, perhaps remembers Aristophanes in one phrase:

> "Then wrong it were that any other twaine
> Should in loves gentle band combyned bee
> But those whom heaven did at first ordaine,
> And made out of one mould the more t' agree.
>   *Hymn* II. (ll. 204—207).

---

[1] See Introduction III.   [2] *Symposium* 192.
[3] See Introduction III.

Aristophanes dwells on the danger of man's being again split up if he becomes rebellious and proud, but once more grows serious:

"My words have a wider application—they include men and women everywhere, and I believe that if our loves were perfectly accomplished and each one, returning to his primaeval nature, had his original true love, then our race would be happy. And if this would be best of all, the best in the next degree and under present circumstances must be the nearest approach to such a union; and that will be the attainment of a congenial love."

λέγω δὲ οὖν ἔγωγε καθ᾽ ἁπάντων καὶ ἀνδρῶν καὶ γυναικῶν, ὅτι οὕτως ἂν ἡμῶν τὸ γένος εὔδαιμον γένοιτο, εἰ ἐκτελέσαιμεν τὸν ἔρωτα καὶ τῶν παιδικῶν τῶν αὑτοῦ ἕκαστος τύχοι εἰς τὴν ἀρχαίαν ἀπελθὼν φύσιν [1].

So with Spenser:

"But, in your choice of Loves, this well advize,
 That likest to your selves ye them select,
 The which your forms first sourse may sympathize,
 And with like beauties parts be inly deckt;
 For, if you loosely love without respect,
 It is no love, but a discordant warre,
 Whose unlike parts amongst themselves do jarre."

Hymn II. (ll. 190—196).

The speech of Agathon declares that love, so far from being the eldest of the gods, is, in reality, the youngest and tenderest [2].

Spenser does not trouble to reconcile this with the speech of Phaedrus which had stated that love was the eldest of the gods, nor does he fully accept Ficino's method of reconciling the opposed statements [3] but he simply lays them side by side :

"Though elder then thine owne nativitie,
 And yet a chyld, renewing still thy yeares,
 And yet the eldest of the heavenly Peares."

Hymn I. (ll. 54—56).

[1] *Symposium* 193. [2] See also notes p. 45.
[3] See Introduction III.

Socrates, in making his speech, will not claim the credit for it himself but declares himself to have been taught by a wise woman—Diotima of Mantineia. Diotima narrates a parable concerning the birth of Love who, she says, was born on the birthday of Aphrodite; his father was the god Poros or Plenty, and his mother Penia or Poverty, but he is the follower of Aphrodite, partly because he was born on her birthday, and partly because he is a lover of the beautiful, and Aphrodite herself is beautiful[1].

This idea also Spenser tries to adopt but does not succeed in making it consistent; he wishes to keep to the ordinary conception, expressed in the previous speeches of the *Symposium* that Love is the child of Aphrodite, and recognises the other idea only in a very inconsistent manner:

> " Or who alive can perfectly declare
> The wondrous cradle of thine infancie,
> When thy great mother Venus first thee bare,
> Begot of Plentie and of Penurie."
>
> *Hymn* I. (ll. 50—54).

He does not suggest how it is possible for both to be true.

Having spoken of the nature and birth of love and declared that love is love of the beautiful, Diotima goes on to put the question more clearly and asks: " When a man loves the beautiful what does he desire?" She explains fully that love is the desire, not of beauty, but of birth in beauty, and the birth may be either of body or of soul:

" I mean to say that all men are bringing to the birth in their bodies and in their souls. There is a certain age at which human nature is desirous of procreation—procreation which must be in beauty and not in deformity; and this procreation is the union of man and woman and is a divine thing; for conception and generation are an immortal principle in the mortal creature and in the inharmonious they can never be. But the deformed is always inharmonious with the divine and the beautiful harmonious. Beauty, then, is the destiny or goddess of parturition who presides at birth, and therefore, when

[1] *Symposium* 203.

approaching beauty the conceiving power is propitious, and diffuse, and benign, and begets and bears fruit....

"And this the reason why, when the hour of conception arrives, and the teeming nature is full, there is such a flutter and ecstasy about beauty whose approach is the alleviation of the pain of travail. For love, Socrates, is not, as you imagine, the love of the beautiful only."

κυοῦσιν γάρ, ἔφη, πάντες ἄνθρωποι καὶ κατὰ τὸ σῶμα καὶ κατὰ τὴν ψυχήν, καὶ ἐπειδὰν ἔν τινι ἡλικίᾳ γένωνται, τίκτειν ἐπιθυμεῖ ἡμῶν ἡ φύσις. τίκτειν δὲ ἐν μὲν αἰσχρῷ οὐ δύναται, ἐν δὲ τῷ καλῷ. (ἡ γὰρ ἀνδρὸς καὶ γυναικὸς συνουσία τόκος ἐστίν)....διὰ ταῦτα ὅταν μὲν καλῷ προσπελάζῃ τὸ κυοῦν, ἵλεών τε γίγνεται καὶ εὐφραινόμενον διαχεῖται καὶ τίκτει τε καὶ γεννᾷ·...ὅθεν δὴ τῷ κυοῦντί τε καὶ ἤδη σπαργῶντι πολλὴ ἡ πτοίησις γέγονε περὶ τὸ καλὸν διὰ τὸ μεγάλης ὠδῖνος ἀπολύειν τὸν ἔχοντα· ἔστιν γάρ, ἔφη, οὐ τοῦ καλοῦ ὁ ἔρως, ὡς σὺ οἴει.

'Αλλὰ τί μήν;

Τῆς γεννήσεως καὶ τοῦ τόκου ἐν τῷ καλῷ[1].

"To the mortal generation is a sort of eternity and immortality and if, as has already been admitted, love is of the everlasting possession of the good, all men will necessarily desire immortality together with good. Wherefore love is of immortality."

ὅτι ἀειγενές ἐστι καὶ ἀθάνατον ὡς θνητῷ ἡ γέννησις· ἀθανασίας δὲ ἀναγκαῖον ἐπιθυμεῖν μετὰ ἀγαθοῦ ἐκ τῶν ὡμολογημένων, εἴπερ τοῦ ἀγαθοῦ ἑαυτῷ εἶναι ἀεὶ ἔρως ἐστίν. ἀναγκαῖον δὴ ἐκ τούτου τοῦ λόγου καὶ τῆς ἀθανασίας τὸν ἔρωτα εἶναι[2].

"What is the cause of love and the attendant desire? See you not how all animals, birds as well as beasts, in their desire for procreation, are in agony when they take the infection of love, which begins with the desire of union."

"Here again...the mortal nature is seeking, as far as possible, to be everlasting and immortal; and this is only to be attained by generation, because generation always leaves behind a new existence in the place of the old[3]."

[1] *Symposium* 206.   [2] *Ib.* 206, 207.   [3] *Ib.* 207.

Socrates proceeds to distinguish carefully between the men whose bodies only are creative and the men whose souls are creative; the latter, like the former, wander about seeking beauty in order that they may beget offspring, but they are attracted only by the fair and noble and well nurtured soul; in contact with that they bring forth what they have conceived long before, children of the mind, such poems as those of Homer and Hesiod, such laws as those of Lycurgus and Solon.

Spenser does not attempt to mark this distinction, for he is speaking essentially of the love of woman and is not driven to make a sharp contrast between the physical and the intellectual.   Socrates explains that even the animals have a desire for immortality in their way, but Spenser limits this to man.   In other respects the parallel is very close:

> "So ever since they firmly have remained,
>   And duly well observed his beheast;
>   Through which now all these things that are contained
>   Within this goodly cope, both most and least,
>   Their being have, and dayly are increast
>   Through secret sparks of his infused fyre,
>   Which in the barraine cold he doth inspyre.
>
> Thereby they all do live and moved are
>   To multiply the likenesse of their kynd
>   .   .   .   .
> But man that breathes a more immortall mynd,
>   Not for lusts sake, but for eternitie,
>   Seekes to enlarge his lasting progenie;
>   For, having yet in his deducted spright
>   Some sparks remaining of that heavenly fyre,
>   .   .   .   .
> Therefore in choice of love he doth desyre
>   That seemes on earth most heavenly to embrace,
>   That same is Beautie, borne of heavenly race.
>   .   .   .   .
> What wonder then, if with such rage extreme
>   Fraile men, whose eyes seek heavenly things to see,
>   At sight thereof so much enravisht bee?"
>
> *Hymn* I. (ll. 92—119).

Socrates proceeds to explain what he (or rather Diotima) terms the greater mysteries of love.

" He who would proceed aright in this matter should begin in youth to visit beautiful forms ; and first, if he be guided by his instructor aright, to love one such form only, out of that he should create fair thoughts ; and soon he will himself perceive that the beauty of one form is akin to the beauty of another ; and then, if beauty of form in general is his pursuit, how foolish would he not be to recognise that the beauty in every form is one and the same ! and when he perceives this, he will abate his violent love of the one which he will despise, and deem a small thing and will become a lover of all beautiful forms ; in the next stage he will consider that the beauty of the mind is more honourable than the beauty of the outward form. So that if a virtuous soul have but a little comeliness he will be content to love and tend him...and after laws and institutions he will go on to the sciences, that he may see their beauty, being not like a servant in love with the beauty of one youth, or man, or institution...but drawing towards and contemplating the vast sea of beauty, he will create many fair and noble thoughts and notions in boundless love of wisdom until...at last the vision is revealed to him of a single science which is the science of beauty everywhere[1]."

" He who has been instructed thus far in the things of love, and who has learned to see the beautiful in due order and succession, when he comes towards the end will suddenly perceive a nature of wonderful beauty (and this is the final cause of all our former toils) a nature which in the first place is everlasting, not growing or decaying or waxing and waning...but beauty only, absolute, separate, simple, and everlasting, which without diminution and without increase or any change, is imparted to the ever growing and perishing beauties of all other things.... And the true order of going or being led by another to the things of love, is to use the beauties of earth as steps along which he mounts upwards for the sake of that other beauty

[1] *Symposium* 209. For parallel passages in the original see notes pp. 68, 70.

going from one to two, and from two to all fair forms...until
he arrives at the notion of absolute beauty, and at last knows
what the essence of beauty is....But what if man had eyes to
see the true beauty, I mean, pure and clear and unalloyed, not
clogged with the pollutions of mortality and all the colours and
vanities of human life...thither looking and holding converse
with the true beauty divine and simple....Do you not see that,
in that communion only, he will become the friend of God and
be immortal if mortal man may[1]."

It will be seen that this is very closely akin to the con-
ception of love expressed in the *Phaedrus*, is, in fact, another
aspect of the same thing. The difference lies in the method
of approach; in the *Phaedrus* the influence of beauty is the
thing that is to be explained, and it is accounted for by
ascribing it to the reminiscence, wakened by beauty, of the
divine ideas.

In the *Symposium* the method of approach is not primarily
through beauty but through love; love is explained as the
desire of birth in beauty, it is essentially the desire of propaga-
tion, but this propagation is a kind of self-preservation on a
larger scale, it is the longing for immortality, for perpetuation
in various ways. Diotima does not explain why beauty should
be propitious to the creative power, she only says that it is and
that deformity is unpropitious. The crude sort of love, such as
belongs to animals and to sensuous men, is limited to the body,
begets physical offspring and perpetuates the individual by
repetition of the type; the nobler love is of the mind, it causes
inspiration and excites to all kinds of intellectual production:
besides this it leads the mind by gradual stages until it arrives
at a view of the supreme and highest beauty which is incor-
ruptible and unchangeable.

The peculiar feature of the *Symposium* lies in its insistence
on the definite stages or grades traversed by the lover of beauty,
and in the finally beatific vision of the highest beauty. This
conception, one of the most spiritual to be found in Plato, is

---

[1] *Symposium* 211, 212. See also notes p. 70.

used by Spenser mostly in the two later hymns. Spenser
identifies God with the highest beauty spoken of by Plato, he
also takes the Christian idea that God is love; uniting the two
he arrives at the conception that God loves Himself because
He Himself is fair and thus, bringing to birth in his own
beauty, He produces the whole of creation.   Plato's explana-
tion of the creative and generative act of man is applied to
the creative act in God Himself:

> "That High Eternall Powre, which now doth move
> In all these things, mov'd in it selfe by love.
>
> It lov'd it selfe, because it selfe was faire;
> (For faire is lov'd;) and of it selfe begot,
> Like to it selfe his eldest sonne and heire."
>
> *Hymn* III. (ll. 27—31).

In the same way are begotten the Holy Spirit and the
angels.

> "Yet being pregnant still with powrefull grace,
> And full of fruitfull love, that loves to get
> Things like himselfe, and to enlarge his race,
> His second brood, though not in powre so great,
> Yet full of beautie, next he did beget
> An infinite increase of Angels bright."
>
> .   .   .   .   (ll. 50—55.)

It is in the same way that God creates man: (ll. 99—105).

The excellence of man lies in reciprocating the divine love
that has been bestowed upon him and, since Spenser identifies
Plato's supreme beauty with the supreme love, he finds in
Plato imagery to describe the rapture of man's union with
the divine.

> "All other loves, with which the world doth blind.
> Weake fancies, and stirre up affections base,
> Thou must renounce and utterly displace,
>
> .   .   .   .
>
> Then shalt thou feele thy spirit so possest,
> And ravisht with devouring great desire
> Of his deare selfe, that shall thy feeble brest
> Inflame with love, and set thee all on fire
>
> .   .   .   .
>
> That in no earthly thing thou shalt delight,
> But in his sweet and amiable sight.

> Thenceforth all worlds desire will in thee dye,
> And all earthes glorie, on which men do gaze,
> Seeme durt and drosse in thy pure-sighted eye,
> Compar'd to that celestiall beauties blaze,
> Whose glorious beames all fleshly sense doth daze
> With admiration of their passing light,
>
> .   .   .   .
>
> Then shall thy ravisht soule inspired bee
> With heavenly thoughts farre above humane skil,
> And thy bright radiant eyes shall plainely see
> Th' Idee of his pure glorie present still
> Before thy face, that all thy spirits shall fill
> With sweete enragement of celestiall love,
> Kindled through sight of those faire things above."
>
> *Hymn* III. (ll. 262—287).

In the *Hymne of Heavenly Beautie* the fundamental idea is to be found in Plato's conception of the beauties of earth as leading up by stages to the vision of divine beauty.

> " Beginning then below, with th' easie vew
> Of this base world, subject to fleshly eye,
> From thence to mount aloft, by order dew,
> To contemplation of th' immortall sky."
>
> *Hymn* IV. (ll. 22—25).

The whole frame of nature is considered to provide examples of loveliness by which the mind is led up from earthly to heavenly things, and from heavenly things to those of God. The actual stages in this ascent in order of beauty are taken by Spenser from Ficino[1], but the foundation of the whole is Platonism.

> " Then looke, who list thy gazefull eyes to feed
> With sight of that is faire, looke on the frame
> Of this wyde universe, and therein reed
> The endlesse kinds of creatures which by name
> Thou canst not count......
> And all with admirable beautie deckt."
>
> *Hymn* IV. (ll. 29—35).

[1] See Introduction III.

This gradation of beauty passes from the seen to the unseen world, and the different heavens (like those in Dante's *Paradiso*) increase in brightness and beauty as they ascend.

The culminating point is reached in the divine radiance of God.

Plato had described Wisdom as the most beautiful of all the ideas ; thus Spenser describes her of excelling fairness, and, moreover, as the means by which the highest vision of all is attained.

> " None thereof worthy be, but those whom shee
> Vouchsafeth to her presence to receave,
> And letteth them her lovely face to see,
> Whereof such wondrous pleasures they conceave,
> And sweete contentment, that it doth bereave
> Their soule of sense, through infinite delight,
> And them transport from flesh into the spright.
> In which they see such admirable things,
> As carries them into an extasy,
>
> .   .   .   .
>
> That maketh them all worldly cares forget,
> And onely thinke on that before them set.
> Ne from thenceforth doth any fleshly sense,
> Or idle thoughts of earthly things, remaine ;
>
> .   .   .   .
>
> All other sights but fayned shadowes bee.
>
> .   .   .   .
>
> So full their eyes are of that glorious sight,
>
> .   .   .   .
>
> That in nought else on earth they can delight
> But in th' aspect of that felicitie.
>
> .   .   .   .
>
> Ah, then, my hungry soule ! which long hast fed
> On idle fancies of thy foolish thought,
>
> .   .   .   .
>
> Ah ! ceasse to gaze on matter of thy grief :
> And looke at last up to that Soveraine Light,
> From whose pure beams al perfect beauty springs."
>
> *Hymn* IV. (ll. 253—296).

There are not many references in the *Fowre Hymnes* to Platonic dialogues other than the *Phaedrus* and *Symposium*, but a few may be traced elsewhere. *The Hymne in Honour of Beautie* borrows something from the *Timaeus*. In the *Timaeus* it is stated that the artificer who looks always to the abiding and unchangeable, and who fashions his work after an immortal pattern, must of necessity make that work fair and perfect, while the artificer who works only after a created pattern cannot make it perfect. Which pattern had the artificer in view when he made the world? It is evident that it must have been the eternal pattern for the world is fair and perfect[1].

So Spenser:

> "What time this world's great Work-maister did cast
> To make al things such as we now behold,
> It seemes that he before his eyes had plast
> A goodly Paterne, to whose perfect mould
> He fashioned them as comely as he could,
> That now so faire and seemely they appeare,
> As nought may be amended any wheare."
>
> *Hymn* II. (ll. 29—35).

Spenser does not, it is true, fully understand the conception and identifies this world pattern or archetype with Plato's idea of beauty which is plainly not the case:

> "That wondrous Paterne, wheresoere it bee,
> Whether in earth layd up in secret store,
> Or else in heaven, that no man may it see
>
> .   .   .   .
> Is perfect Beautie, which all men adore."
>
> (ll. 36—40.)

From the *Timaeus* Spenser takes his idea of the creation of man who also is made according to a divine pattern:

> "Therefore of clay, base, vile, and next to nought,
> Yet form'd by wondrous skill, and by His might,
> According to an heavenly patterne wrought,
> Which He had fashion in his wise foresight,
> He man did make..."
>
> *Hymn* III. (ll. 106—110).

In the *Timaeus* also there is the conception of the primordial chaos from which the four elements are made.

[1] See also notes pp. 54, 64.

The account of the fate of the just man as given in the *Republic* probably suggested one reference in Spenser's description of the life of Christ.

> "And slew the Just by most unjust decree."
>
> *Hymn* III. (l. 154)[1].

In Book VII. of the *Republic* there occurs an identification of the Form or Idea of Good with all that is highest; it is compared to the sun and the illumination it gives to the marvellous illumination of light whose nature is a mystery :

"I think you will admit that the sun ministers to visible objects, not only the faculty of being seen, but also their vitality, growth and nutriment, though it is not itself equivalent to vitality."

"In like manner the objects of knowledge not only derive from the good the gift of being known, but are further endowed by it with a real and essential existence ; though the good, far from being identical with real existence, actually transcends it.

"In the world of knowledge, the Idea of Good is the limit of our inquiries, and can barely be perceived; but, when perceived, we cannot help concluding that it is in every case the source of all that is bright and beautiful,—in the visible world giving birth to light and its master[2], and in the intellectual world dispensing, immediately and with full authority, truth and reason,—and that whosoever would act wisely, either in private or in public, must set the Idea of Good before his eyes."

We may compare with Spenser :

> "Light, farre exceeding that bright blazing sparke
> Which darted is from Titans flaming head,
>
> .   .   .   .
>
> Whose nature yet so much is marvelled
> Of mortall wits, that it doth much amaze
> The greatest wisards which thereon do gaze.
>
> But that immortall light, which there doth shine,
> Is many thousand times more bright, more cleare,
>
> .   .   .   .
>
> For from th' Eternall Truth it doth proceed,
> Through heavenly vertue which her beames doe breed."
>
> *Hymn* IV. (ll. 162—175).

---

[1] See also notes p. 66.   [2] *i.e.* 'the sun.'

W.

III.

The Influence of Ficino and Bruno on The "Fowre Hymnes."

It is unquestionable that the Italian Platonists influenced Spenser considerably for many of their ideas are to be found in his works, in different portions of *The Faerie Queene* as well as in the *Fowre Hymnes*.

The most probable channels of this influence were Marsilio Ficino and Giordano Bruno.

Ficino, as already explained, was the chief exponent of Platonism for the whole of the Italian Renaissance; he translated Plato into Latin and wrote a treatise on his doctrine of immortality, he also translated Plotinus.

It is practically certain that Spenser who drew so much from the *Symposium* would read Ficino's commentary upon it, the *Commentarium in Convivium*, and what on *à priori* grounds is almost certain becomes confirmed when we lay the two side by side, and see how close are the resemblances between them.

It is probable also that Spenser knew Giordano Bruno's erotic treatise *De gl' heroici furori*. The fragment of the seventh book of *The Faerie Queene*, the cantos on Mutability, owes its main inspiration to Bruno, thus proving that Spenser knew and read his philosophical works. The essay *De gl' heroici furori*, was written while Bruno was in England and published in the year 1585, dedicated to Sir Philip Sidney.

Ficino and Bruno contain much the same ideas, the foundation in both cases being Platonism but their method is different.

Ficino, as the title of his work implies, bases everything directly on the *Symposium*; he takes each one of the speeches contained in it and analyses them in turn; he then, in subsequent chapters, discusses and illustrates Plato's meaning in the light of the Neo-Platonists, and of Plotinus in especial, and also devotes his whole energies to show that Plato is in harmony with Christian ideas.

Bruno, in his erotic treatise, writes more immediately and personally as if expressing his own views on love. He begins by marvelling at the sway of this passion, the power it is able to exercise over all men, driving even the most intellectual to a kind of madness and filling them with jealousy and despair. There seems to be, Bruno says, something ignoble in this but it is not really so. Beauty possesses its power over a man because it is the embodiment of a beautiful soul, and this soul in its turn is a revelation of the divine; love thus educates the whole mind and soul of the lover, it exalts and inspires him, makes him capable of understanding all that is most noble on earth and finally of apprehending the world beyond. The excitement produced by beauty is not a mere excitement of sense, laying ignoble chains on the individual, it is the most inspiring motive in human life.

Throughout the essay the essential topic is the Platonic doctrine of ascent by stages, ascent from sense perception and the feeling for physical beauty to reverence for the soul, and from reverence for the soul to the ecstatic vision and love of the divine beauty.

It will be remembered that in the *Symposium* Phaedrus stated love to be the eldest of the gods while Agathon maintained that love was the youngest. Ficino devotes a whole division of his commentary (v. 10) to reconciling these discrepancies. He explains them by saying that the love by which the angelic bodies were created is older than they, but the love by which the creation is maintained is younger. Spenser simply puts the ideas side by side without explaining them, but he had Ficino's warrant that both views were true.

> "Though elder then thine own nativitie,
> And yet a chyld, renewing still thy yeares,
> And yet the eldest of the heavenly Peares."
>
> *Hymn* 1. (ll. 54—56).

The speech of Eryximachus had stated that love is present in all things, in all animals as well as in man. Ficino developes this in his commentary by representing love as the creator and preserver of all things.

It is love which binds together all portions of the earth;
earth, water, and air, are all held and preserved in their places
by the force of love; they are preserved by love which
maintains the unity of their parts, and when this unity is
destroyed they perish (III. 2).

"Ejusdem enim semper est affectionis et conservationis officium.
Nempe similia similibus conservantur. Amor autem simile ad simile
trahit. Terrae partes singulae amore mutuo copulante, ad partes alias
terrae sui similes sese conservunt. Tota enim terra ad simile sibi mundi
centrum illius aviditate descendit. Aquae partes ad sese invicem
similiter et ad locum sibi convenientem cum toto aquae corpore ser-
vuntur. Idem partes aeris ignisque...ac etiam duo haec elementa ad
supernam regionem sibi congruam et similem regionis illius amore
trahuntur. Coelum etiam, ut Plato inquit, innato movetur amore....
Quinetiam unitate partium suarum cuncta servantur, dispersione par-
tium pereunt. Unitatem vero partium mutuus earundem efficit
amor[1]."

Love not only preserves all things, but is also the creative
principle. It is a desire of propagating implanted in all
creation. Absolute perfection is contained in God; the divine
intelligence contemplating this desired to propagate it beyond
itself; from this desire arose the universe, and hence the same
desire for propagation was from the beginning implanted in
the whole universe.

"Secundum vero illud nostrae orationis membrum, quo amor effector
omnium et servator est dictus, ita probatur. Cupiditas perfectionis
proprie propagandae amor quidam est. Absoluta perfectio, in summa
dei est potentia. Eam divina intelligentia contemplatur, atque inde
voluntas eadem cupit extra se propagare : ex quo propagandi amore
creata ab eo sunt omnia. Idcirco Dionysius noster Divinus, inquit,
amor non permisit regem omnium sine germine in seipso manere.
Idem propagationis instinctus omnibus ab illo primo autore est inditus.
Per hunc sancti illius spiritus coelos movent et sequentibus omnibus
sua munera largiuntur....Herbae quoque ac arbores cupidae sui seminis
propagandi sui similia gignunt. Animalia quoque, bruta et homines
ejusdem cupiditatis illecebris ad procreandum sobolem rapiuntur.
Quod si amor omnia facit, servat etiam omnia[2]."

[1] See also notes p. 46.

[2] Ficino *Commentarium in Convivium* III. 2. See also notes p. 47.

So he says (III. 3) that all portions of the world are the works of one artificer, they are parts, as it were, of a mechanism which are bound together by a certain mutual love, so that love may be declared to be the perpetual bond of the universe, the unmoving support and firm basis of the whole[1].

We may compare this with Spenser (*Hymn* I.):

> " The world, that was not till he did it make,
>   Whose sundrie parts he from themselves did sever
>   The which before had lyen confused ever.
>
>   The earth, the ayre, the water, and the fyre,
>   Then gan to raunge them selves in huge array,
>   And with contràry forces to conspyre
>   Each against other by all meanes they may,
>   Threatning their owne confusion and decay :
>   Ayre hated earth, and water hated fyre,
>   Till Love relented their rebellious yre.
>
>   He then them tooke, and, tempering goodly well
>   Their contrary dislikes with loved meanes,
>   Did place them all in order, and compell
>   To keepe them selves within their sundrie raines,
>   Together linkt with Adamantine chaines ;
>   Yet so, as that in every living wight
>   They mix themselves, and shew their kindly might."

(ll. 75—91.)

They have ever since remained firmly in their placès, but they are none the less inspired by the force of love ; it is through love that all things

> " Their being have, and dayly are increast
>   Through secret sparks of his infused fyre,
>   Which in the barraine cold he doth inspyre.
>
>   Thereby they all do live, and moved are
>   To multiply the likenesse of their kynd."

(ll. 96—100.)

In the *Hymne in Honour of Beautie* the influence of the Italian Platonists is still more marked. Spenser first outlines a theory of aesthetics which accounts for the presence of beauty in the universe around us.

Ficino and Bruno both explain beauty as a spiritual thing,

---

[1] For original passage see notes p. 46.

the splendour of God's light shining in the world; the whole
universe is an emanation from God and His divine light shines,
more or less, in all matter.

Beauty, says Ficino (v. 4), is splendour. It penetrates all
things, being more brilliant as they are nearer God. Beauty
is a certain vivacity and brightness infused in matter; it is
something incorporeal and is never inherent in matter itself;
it is infused by God first into angels, next into the minds of
men and from the mind into the body; through the appeal
of sight it moves and delights our minds and inflames them
with love.

"Quid tandem est corporis pulchritudo? Actus vivacitas, et gratia
quaedam ideae suae influxu in ipso refulgens....Caeterum ne longius
digrediatur oratio, ex supradictis breviter concludamus; pulchritudinem
esse gratiam quandam vivacem et spiritalem, dei ratio, illustrante angelo
primum infusam: inde et animis hominum, corporumque: ...quae per
rationem, visum,...animos nostros movet atque delectat, delectando
capit, rapiendo inflammat amore[1]."

Beauty, Ficino argues, is something incorporeal because it
can be found not only in material things, but in things such
as sounds and qualities. Even when we speak of bodies as
beautiful they are not beautiful by virtue of their material
because, as we see, the same body may be beautiful to-day
and deformed and plain to-morrow. Therefore beauty is
something other than the body itself. There are some who
say that beauty arises from a certain proportion of parts, or
sweetness, or grace of colour, but this is not true, for beauty
is by no means the same thing as proportion since it is not
possible to say what proportions will give it.

"Cum haec ita se habeant, necessarium est pulchritudinem esse
aliquid virtuti, figurae, vocibusque commune....Quo sit ut ipsa pul-
chritudinis ratio corpus esse non possit: quoniam virtutibus animi quae
incorporeae sunt, pulchritudo si esset corporea, minime conveniret....
Quamvis enim corpora quaedam speciosa dicamus, non tamen sunt
ex ipsa sui materia speciosa. Siquidem corpus hominis unum atque
idem hodie formosum, cras autem casu aliquo foedante deforme: quasi
aliud sit esse corpus, aliud esse formosum. Neque etiam sunt ex ipsa

[1] Ficino v. 6. See also notes p. 55.

quantitate formosa....Eadem nos ratione admonet ne formam sus-
picemur esse colorum suavitatem[1]."

Bruno teaches the same. Beauty is not a corporeal thing;
the beauty which is seen in bodies is something accidental and
shadowy, which can be changed and spoilt by a very little
alteration, so that the same body will cease to be beautiful
and will become ugly[2].

What really fascinates is the light of the spirit showing
itself through the body; if it were the body only then a
picture or statue would do just as well.

"Io mai fui piu fascinato da cosa simile; che potesse al presente
esser fascinato da qualche statua ò pittura, dalle quali mi pare in-
differente[3]."

So with Spenser! He explains how everything is beautiful
in so far as it partakes of the original divine beauty:

> "Thereof as every earthly thing partakes
> Or more or lesse, by influence divine,
> So it more fair accordingly it makes,
> And the grosse matter of this earthly myne
> Which clotheth it thereafter doth refyne.
>
>   .   .   .   .   .
>
> For, through infusion of celestiall powre,
> The duller earth it quickneth with delight,
> And life-full spirits privily doth powre
> Through all the parts, that to the lookers sight
> They seeme to please...
>
> That is the thing which giveth pleasant grace
> To all things faire, that kindleth lively fyre,
> Light of thy lampe; which, shyning in the face,
> Thence to the soule darts amorous desyre.
>
>   .   .   .   .   .
>
> How vainely then doe ydle wits invent,
> That beautie is nought else but mixture made
> Of colours faire, and goodly temp'rament
> Of pure complexions, that shall quickly fade
> And passe away, like to a sommers shade;

---

[1] Ficino v. 3. See also notes pp. 55, 56.
[2] Bruno p. 672. For original see notes p. 56.   [3] Bruno p. 640.

Or that it is but comely composition
Of parts well measurd, with meet disposition !
Hath white and red in it such wondrous powre?

   •   •   •   •   •

Or can proportion of the outward part
Move such affection in the inward mynd?

   •   '   •   •   •   •   •

Why doe not then the blossomes of the field,
Which are arayd with much more orient hew,

   •   •   •   •   •   •

Worke like impression in the lookers vew?
Or why do not faire pictures like powre shew,
In which oft-times we nature see of art
Exceld, in perfect limming every part?

         .. ...there is more then so,
That workes such wonders in the minds of men;
I, that have often prov'd, too well it know."

(ll. 43—87.)

The second part of the hymn explains the true origin of the beauty to be found in the human body. It is essentially due to the formative and creative power of the human soul.

The clearest explanation of this is given by Bruno. He sees that it is the soul which makes the beauty of the body and which has wrought it to be what it is; the body is not beautiful of itself, the body is only the shadow of the soul and the soul is incomparably more beautiful.

"La raggion dumque apprende il piu vero bello per conversione á quello che fá la beltade nel corpo, et viene á formarlo bello, et questa é l' anima che l' há talmente fabricato et infigurato: Appresso l' intelletto s' inalza piu, et apprende bene che l' anima é incomparabilmente bella sopra la bellezza che possa esser ne gli corpi[1]."

Moreover the soul is not locally situated in the body at all, but is in it only as an internal model and an external formative power; it shapes it both within and without[2].

"Every noble love has for its true object divine beauty; this divine beauty communicates itself first to the soul and shines in

[1] Bruno p. 672.
[2] Bruno p. 647. For original see notes p. 58.

that and from that, or rather through and by means of that,
communicates itself to the body ; a really noble affection loves
bodily beauty inasmuch as it is the evidence of beauty of soul.
We love the body because of a certain spirituality we see in it ;
it is this spirituality which is called beauty and which does not
consist in any proportions or in certain colours or forms, but in
the harmony of the whole. This harmony shows an affinity
with the spirit and the most acute senses at once perceive
that."

" Tutti gli amori (si sono heroici...) hanno per oggetto la divinitá,
tendeno alla divina bellezza, la quale prima si comunica all' anime, et
risplende in quelle, et da quelle poi ò (per dir meglo) per quelle poi si
comunica alli corpi : onde é che l' affetto ben formato ama gli corpi ò
la corporale bellezza, per quel che é indice della bellezza del spirito....

" Questa mostra certa sensibile affinitá col spirito á gli sensi piu
acuti et penetrativi[1]."

So with Spenser.

" For that same goodly hew of white and red
      .   .   .   .
Shall turne to dust......
But that faire lampe, from whose celestiall ray
That light proceedes, which kindleth lovers fire,
Shall never be extinguisht nor decay;
For it is heavenly borne and can not die,
Being a parcell of the purest skie.

      .   .   .   .
Which powre retayning still......
When she in fleshly seede is eft enraced,
Through every part she doth the same impresse,
According as the heavens have her graced,
And frames her house, in which she will be placed,
Fit for her selfe,......
Therof it comes that these faire soules, which have
The most resemblance of that heavenly light,
Frame to themselves most beautifull and brave
Their fleshly bowre, most fit for their delight,
And the grosse matter by a soveraine might
Tempers so trim, that it may well be seene
A pallace fit for such a virgin Queene.

[1] Bruno p. 643. See also notes p. 57.

> So every spirit, as it is most pure,
> And hath in it the more of heavenly light,
> So it the fairer bodie doth procure
> To habit in, and it more fairely dight
>
>   .   .   .   .
>
> For of the soule the bodie forme doth take ;
> For soule is forme, and doth the bodie make."
>
> (ll. 92—133.)

The objection at once arises that the body is not, as a matter of fact, in all cases an index to the soul, for it may happen that people of fine character are not particularly beautiful.

Ficino explains this fact by saying that sometimes the matter out of which the soul has to make the body is disobedient and unyielding. One soul may find suitable material upon earth and mould the body rightly according to its first plan ; another, because of the unsuitability of the material, bungles (inchoaverit) or cannot complete its task, and so does not make the body according to its true model[1]."

So Spenser :

> "Yet oft it falles that many a gentle mynd
> Dwels in deformed tabernacle drownd,
> Either by chaunce, against the course of kynd,
> Or through unaptnesse in the substance fownd,
> Which it assumed of some stubborne grownd,
> That will not yield unto her formes direction,
> But is deform'd with some foule imperfection."
>
> (ll. 141—147.)

In the third portion of the *Hymne* Spenser proceeds to explain why it is that beauty has such power over the mind of the lover, and why the lover almost invariably believes the beloved to be more beautiful than is actually the case. Both Ficino and Bruno explain this in detail.

Ficino accepts the mediaeval idea that every soul is born under the ascendency of some star, by which star its whole disposition is influenced. As Ficino puts it

" Whatever soul is born upon earth under the ascendency of Jove (Jupiter) makes for itself a body in which the influence of Jove predominates. The model is first made in aether and afterwards carried out in material form. If the soul finds suitable matter it can mould it

---

[1] Ficino VI. 6. For original see notes pp. 57, 58.

exactly to the type, but if (as already explained) the matter is unsuitable, it is not able to do this. Thus, of two souls born under the ascendency of the same star, one may have a much more beautiful body than the other; nevertheless they love each other because their natures are similar. The lover, however, has the power of beholding in the beloved the true and original nature, and therefore of constructing in his mind's eye the ethereal form which is far more beautiful; it is this image which he always sees and this image which he loves, and therefore lovers so often believe each other far more beautiful than they are."

" Quicunque animus sub Jovis imperio in terrenum corpus delabitur, certam quandam in ipso descensu sibi concipit hominis fabricandi figuram Jovis astro convenientem. Hanc in aethereo sui corpore tanquam optime affecto exprimit exactissimam. Si nactus in terris semen fuerit similiter temperatum, in eo quoque tertiam figuram pingit, primae secundaeque simillimam. Sin contrà, non ita persimilem[1]....

" Corpus illud isto formosius. Ambo sibi propter quandam naturae similitudinem mutuo placent....

"Proinde qui, ut diximus, eodem sunt astro sub orti, ita se habent, ut pulchrioris eorum simulacrum, per oculos in alterius animam manans, consimili cuidam simulachro, tam in corpore aethereo, quam in animi penetralibus ab ipsa generatione formato quadret, et undique consonet. Ita pulsatus animus obvium illud simulacrum tanquam suum aliquid recognoscit....

" Hinc accidit, ut amantes ita decipiantur : ut formosiorem quam sit, existiment. Nam procedente tempore amatum non in mera ejus imagine per sensus accepta perspiciunt : sed in simulacro iam ab anima ad ideae suae similitudinem reformato, quod ipso corpore pulchrius est, intuentur[2]."

Bruno does not give the same explanation, but he also insists that what the lover really loves is not the actual outward form, but the more refined form he presents to his own mind.

It is not the outward form or visible appearance which has any power of moving in itself; it is not while the lover stands admiring the figure presented to his eyes that he loves but when his mind conceives in itself an image, not visible but present to the thought (non piu visibile ma cogitabile), not as an actual thing but as an idea or type of the good and the beautiful, it is at that moment love is born[3].

[1] See also notes p. 57.   [2] See also notes p. 58.   Ficino VI. 6.
[3] Bruno p. 658.   For original see notes p. 60.

Spenser adopts the explanations :

" For Love is a celestiall harmonie
Of likely harts composd of starres concent,
Which joyne together in sweete sympathie,
To worke ech others joy and true content,
Which they have harbourd since their first descent
Out of their heavenly bowres, where they did see
And know ech other here belov'd to bee.

Then wrong it were that any other twaine
Should in loves gentle band combyned bee
But those whom heaven did at first ordaine,
And made out of one mould the more t' agree ;
For all, that like the beautie which they see,
Streight do not love ; for Love is not so light
As streight to burne at first beholders sight.

But they, which love indeede, looke otherwise,
With pure regard and spotlesse true intent,
Drawing out of the object of their eyes
A more refyned forme, which they present
Unto their mind, voide of all blemishment ;
Which it reducing to her first perfection,
Beholdeth free from fleshes frayle infection.

And then conforming it unto the light,
Which in it selfe it hath remaining still,
.   .   .   .   .
Thereof he fashions in his higher skill
An heavenly beautie to his fancies will
And, it embracing in his mind entyre,
The mirrour of his owne thought doth admyre.

Which seeing now so inly faire to be,
As outward it appeareth to the eye,
And with his spirits proportion to agree,
He thereon fixeth all his fantasie,
And fully setteth his felicitie ;
Counting it fairer then it is indeede,
And yet indeede her fairenesse doth exceede.

For lovers eyes more sharply sighted bee
Than other mens,......
And to their eyes that inmost faire display,
As plaine as light discovers dawning day." (ll. 197—238.)

The *Hymne of Heavenly Beautie* also shows very strongly the influence of Ficino and Bruno.

Ficino says that the divine power first proved itself by creating the angels and then the rest of the world ; it shows itself much more completely in those things which are near to it, and in the order and disposition of the whole world, than in the material of the world itself ; it shines most brightly in the angels and in human souls, next brightly in the sun, and moon, and the stars, next in the elements, and finally in stones, and trees, and animals. The Platonic ideas or types reveal themselves plainly in the orb of earth, more plainly in the mind of man, and most plainly in the mind of the angels. It is, however, the same countenance of God which reveals itself in all these things, in the angels, in the soul of man, and in the frame of the world ; it is clearest and brightest in those things which are nearest to him and darkest in the more remote ; in the outermost things it is very dark if we compare them with the rest.

"Divina potestas omnia supereminens statim à se natis angelis, atque animis suum illum radium in quo secunda vis inest omnium creandorum, tanque filiis infundit. Hic in eis utpote sibi propinquioribus totius mundi dispositionem et ordinem multo pingit exactius quam in mundi materia. Quamobrem haec mundi pictura quam cernimus universa, in angelis et animis lucet expressior. In illis enim sphaerae cujusque figura, solis, lunae, et syderum reliquorum, elementorum quoque, lapidum, arborum, animalium singulorum. Picturae hujusmodi in angelis exemplaria et ideae: in animis rationes et notiones ; imagines à Platonicis nominantur ; clarae quidem in orbe : clariores in animo: in angeli mente clarissimae. Unus igitur dei vultus tribus deinceps per ordinem positis lucet in speculis, Angelo, Animo, Corpore mundi. In illo tanquam propinquiore clarissime : in hoc remotiore obscurius : in hoc remotissimo, si ad caetera compares obscurissime[1]."

Again Ficino says that there is the same beauty visible in all things because they all have the same origin ; God is the Maker of the whole and daily communicates his beauty to angels and spirits and to the whole material of the world. The true reason of all beauty is in God.

[1] Ficino v. 4.

"Quod autem unum est, ab uno debet oriri. Quapropter una multorum corporum pulchritudo ab uno aliquo incorporali pendet artifice. Artifex unus omnium Deus est, qui per angelos atque animas pulchram quotidie reddit omnem mundi materiam. Propterea veram illam pulchritudinis rationem in Deo ejusque[1]."

Spenser accepts this explanation. All things reveal the same beauty : the earth, the elements, the stars, the sun and moon, and beyond them the heavens and the angels ; all are more beautiful in order as they approach to God.

"First, th' Earth, on adamantine pillers founded
. . . .
Then th' Aire still flitting, but yet firmely bounded
On everie side, with pyles of flaming brands,
. . . . . .
By view whereof it plainly may appeare,
That still as every thing doth upward tend,
And further is from earth, so still more cleare
And faire it growes, till to his perfect end
Of purest beautie it at last ascend.
. . . .
Looke then no further, but affixe thine eye
On that bright shynie round still moving Masse,
. . . . . .
All sowd with glistring stars more thicke then grasse,
Whereof each other doth in brightnesse passe,
But those two most, which, ruling night and day,
As King and Queene, the heavens Empire sway ;
. . . .
For farre above these heavens, which here we see,
Be others farre exceeding these in light,
. . . . . .
Faire is the heaven where happy soules have place,
In full enjoyment of felicitie.
. . . . . .
More faire is that, where those Idees on hie
Enraunged be, which Plato so admyred,
And pure Intelligences from God inspyred.
. . . .
Yet fairer then they both, and much more bright,
Be th' Angels and Archangels, which attend
On Gods owne person, without rest or end.

[1] Ficino VI. 18.

These thus in faire each other farre excelling,
As to the Highest they approch more neare,
Yet is that Highest farre beyond all telling,
Fairer then all the rest which there appeare

    .   .   .   .

Those unto all he daily doth display,
And shew himselfe in th' image of his grace,
As in a looking-glasse, through which he may
Be seene of all his creatures vile and base.

                  (ll. 36—116.)

Bruno also shows how all beauty in external things leads the soul up to the vision of divine beauty:

"Why should we make mention of any earthly object when the true object is divinity itself: that is the final object, the last and most perfect, not as we see it in this world where we can see God only, as it were, in shadow and in a mirror; we do not apprehend Him as we apprehend bodily beauty by reason of the senses but in the mind itself. We thus lose our love and desire for all other things, either things that can be perceived by the senses or by the mind, and become wholly penetrated with God....The human intellect feeds itself upon the images and appearances of the lower world only till it can perceive the beauty of the divinity....In this world we see the divine beauty only indirectly by means of its effects, in shadows, and as it were, in images, but in the other world we shall see it in itself as it truly is."

"Come dumque fá mentione di quella specie per oggetto, se (come mi pare) il vero oggétto é la divinitá istessa?

"La è oggetto finale, ultimo et perfettissimo : non gia in questo stato dove non possemo veder dio se non come in ombra et specchio...ma quel puó esser formata nella mente per virtú de l' intelletto. Nel qual stato ritrovandosi viene á perder l' amore et affection d' ogni altra cosa tanto sensibile quanto intelligibile[1]."

If, Bruno says, that beauty which is only a shadow, and belongs merely to the outward appearance of matter, can so move and impress the mind, what will it not be with that which is absolutely beautiful of itself: the contemplation of it will inspire the mind to transform itself and unite with it.

"Oime (dirá) se una bellezza umbratile, fosca...depinta nella superficie de la materia corporale, tanto mi piace...et mi s' attira...che di quello che sustanzialmente, originalmente, primitivamente é bello...

[1] Bruno p. 646. See also notes pp. 72, 73, 76.

conviene dumque che la contemplatione di questo vestigio di luce mi
amene mediante la ripurgation de l' animo mio all' imitatione, con-
formitá, et participatione di quella piu degna et alta, in cui mi
transforme et á cui mi unisca: perche son certo che la natura che
mi há messa questa bellezza avanti gl' occhi...vogla ch' io da quà
basso vegna promosso á l' altezza et eminenza di specie piu eccellenti[1]."

This is the same gradation of beauty as in Spenser's hymn :

> "how can we see with feeble eyne
> The glory of that Majestie Divine?
>
> .   .   .   .
>
> The meanes, therefore, which unto us is lent
> Him to behold, is on his workes to looke,
> Which he hath made in beauty excellent
>
> .   .   .   .
>
> For all thats good is beautifull and faire."
>
> (ll. 123—133.)

By Sapience, or Wisdom, they are admitted to a sight of
the divine beauty.

> "That maketh them all worldly cares forget,
> And onely thinke on that before them set.
>
> Ne from thenceforth doth any fleshly sense,
> Or idle thought of earthly things, remaine ;
>
> .   .   .   .
>
> All other sights but fayned shadowes bee.
>
> .   .   .   .
>
> So full their eyes are of that glorious sight,
>
> .   .   .   .
>
> That in nought else on earth they can delight."
>
> (ll. 265—283.)

[1] Bruno p 694.

NOTE.—Spenser's works seem to show two main periods of Platonic influence,
one early (*Shepheards Calender* and *Faerie Queene*, Bk I.) which consists of
Platonism pure and simple and the other later (*Faerie Queene*, Bk VII. and *Amoretti*)
in which the Platonism is largely tinged with Neo-Platonism.   Spenser himself
declares that the first two 'Hymnes' were composed "in the greener times of my
youth," and in the "Hymne of Heavenly Love" he speaks of having made "many
lewd layes" in praise of love; but in his earliest published work, *The Shepheards
Calender* (1579), he already speaks of himself as being past his youth and he is cer-
tainly already a somewhat severe Puritan.   The inference would seem to be that the
two earlier 'Hymnes' belonged to a period of erotic poetry but were altered and
amended for publication; the two later 'Hymnes' differ in their mentality, being
fundamentally Neo-Platonist.   It is probable that Spenser often rewrote his early
works, as examples of it appear to have been incorporated in *The Faerie Queene*. See
however: *Englische Studien* (1913-14), "The Date of Spenser's Earlier Hymns,"
by Percy N. Long.

FOWRE HYMNES,

MADE BY

EDM. SPENSER.

TO THE RIGHT HONORABLE AND MOST VERTUOUS LADIES,

THE LADIE MARGARET,

COUNTESSE OF CUMBERLAND, AND

THE LADIE MARIE,

COUNTESSE OF WARWICKE.

HAVING in the greener times of my youth, composed these former two Hymnes in the praise of Love and Beautie, and finding that the same too much pleased those of like age and disposition, which being too vehemently caried with that kind of affection, do rather sucke out poyson to their strong passion, then hony to their honest delight, I was moved by the one of you two most excellent Ladies, to call in the same. But, being unable so to doe, by reason that many copies thereof were formerly scattered abroad, I resolved at least to amend, and, by way of retractation, to reforme them, making, in stead of those two Hymnes of earthly or naturall love and beautie, two others of heavenly and celestiall. The which I doe dedicate joyntly unto you two honorable sisters, as to the most excellent and rare ornaments of all true love and beautie, both in the one and the other kinde; humbly beseeching you to vouchsafe the patronage of them, and to accept this my humble service, in lieu of the great graces and honourable favours which ye dayly shew unto me, untill such time as I may, by better meanes, yeeld you some more notable testimonie of my thankfull mind and dutifull devotion. And even so I pray for your happinesse. Greenwich this first of September, 1596. Your Honors most bounden ever,

in all humble service,

ED. SP.

AN HYMNE IN HONOUR OF LOVE.

Love, that long since hast to thy mighty powre
Perforce subdude my poore captivëd hart,
And, raging now therein with restlesse stowre,
Doest tyrannize in everie weaker part;
Faine would I seeke to ease my bitter smart
By any service I might do to thee,
Or ought that else might to thee pleasing bee.

And now t' asswage the force of this new flame,
And make thee more propitious in my need,
I meane to sing the praises of thy name,   10
And thy victorious conquests to areed,
By which thou madest many harts to bleed
Of mighty Victors, with wyde wounds embrewed,
And by thy cruell darts to thee subdewed.

Onely I feare my wits enfeebled late,
Through the sharpe sorrowes which thou hast me bred,
Should faint, and words should faile me to relate
The wondrous triumphs of my great god-hed:
But, if thou wouldst vouchsafe to overspred
Me with the shadow of thy gentle wing,   20
I should enabled be thy actes to sing.

Come, then, O come, thou mightie God of Love,
Out of thy silver bowres and secret blisse,
Where thou doest sit in Venus lap above,
Bathing thy wings in her ambrosiall kisse,
That sweeter farre then any Nectar is;
Come softly, and my feeble breast inspire
With gentle furie, kindled of thy fire.

And ye, sweet Muses! which have often proved
The piercing points of his avengefull darts;   30
And ye, faire Nimphs! which oftentimes have loved
The cruell worker of your kindly smarts,
Prepare your selves, and open wide your harts
For to receive the triumph of your glorie,
That made you merie oft when ye were sorie.

And ye, faire blossomes of youths wanton breed,
Which in the conquests of your beautie bost,
Wherewith your lovers feeble eyes you feed,
But sterve their harts that needeth nourture most,
Prepare your selves to march amongst his host,   40
And all the way this sacred hymne do sing,
Made in the honor of your Soveraigne king.

  GREAT GOD OF MIGHT, that reignest in the mynd,
And all the bodie to thy hest doest frame,
Victor of gods, subduer of mankynd,
That doest the Lions and fell Tigers tame,
Making their cruell rage thy scornefull game,
And in their roring taking great delight;
Who can expresse the glorie of thy might?

Or who alive can perfectly declare   50
The wondrous cradle of thine infancie,
When thy great mother Venus first thee bare,
Begot of Plentie and of Penurie,
Though elder then thine owne nativitie,
And yet a chyld, renewing still thy yeares,
And yet the eldest of the heavenly Peares?

For ere this worlds still moving mightie masse
Out of great Chaos ugly prison crept,
In which his goodly face long hidden was

From heavens view, and in deepe darknesse kept,   60
Love, that had now long time securely slept
In Venus lap, unarmed then and naked,
Gan reare his head, by Clotho being waked:

And, taking to him wings of his owne heate,
Kindled at first from heavens life-giving fyre,
He gan to move out of his idle seate;
Weakely at first, but after with desyre
Lifted aloft, he gan to mount up hyre,
And, like fresh Eagle, make his hardie flight
Through all that great wide wast, yet wanting light.   70

Yet wanting light to guide his wandring way,
His owne faire mother, for all creatures sake,
Did lend him light from her owne goodly ray;
Then through the world his way he gan to take,
The world, that was not till he did it make,
Whose sundrie parts he from themselves did sever
The which before had lyen confused ever.

The earth, the ayre, the water, and the fyre,
Then gan to raunge them selves in huge array,
And with contràry forces to conspyre   80
Each against other by all meanes they may,
Threatning their owne confusion and decay:
Ayre hated earth, and water hated fyre,
Till Love relented their rebellious yre.

He then them tooke, and, tempering goodly well
Their contrary dislikes with loved meanes,
Did place them all in order, and compell
To keepe them selves within their sundrie raines,
Together linkt with Adamantine chaines;
Yet so, as that in every living wight   90
They mixe themselves, and shew their kindly might.

So ever since they firmely have remained,
And duly well observed his beheast;
Through which now all these things that are contained
Within this goodly cope, both most and least,
Their being have, and dayly are increast
Through secret sparks of his infused fyre,
Which in the barraine cold he doth inspyre.

Thereby they all do live, and moved are
To multiply the likenesse of their kynd,   100
Whilest they seeke onely, without further care,
To quench the flame which they in burning fynd;
But man that breathes a more immortall mynd,
Not for lusts sake, but for eternitie,
Seekes to enlarge his lasting progenie;

For, having yet in his deducted spright
Some sparks remaining of that heavenly fyre,
He is enlumind with that goodly light,
Unto like goodly semblant to aspyre;
Therefore in choice of love he doth desyre   110
That seemes on earth most heavenly to embrace,
That same is Beautie, borne of heavenly race.

For sure of all that in this mortall frame
Contained is, nought more divine doth seeme,
Or that resembleth more th' immortall flame
Of heavenly light, then Beauties glorious beame.
What wonder then, if with such rage extreme
Fraile men, whose eyes seek heavenly things to see,
At sight thereof so much enravisht bee?

Which well perceiving, that imperious boy   120
Doth therwith tip his sharp empoisned darts,
Which glancing through the eyes with countenance coy

Rest not till they have pierst the trembling harts,
And kindled flame in all their inner parts,
Which suckes the blood, and drinketh up the lyfe,
Of carefull wretches with consuming griefe.

Thenceforth they playne, and make ful piteous mone
Unto the author of their balefull bane:
The daies they waste, the nights they grieve and grone,
Their lives they loath, and heavens light disdaine;   130
No light but that, whose lampe doth yet remaine
Fresh burning in the image of their eye,
They deigne to see, and seeing it still dye.

That whilst thou tyrant Love doest laugh and scorne
At their complaints, making their paine thy play,
Whylest they lye languishing like thrals forlorne,
The whyles thou doest triumph in their decay;
And otherwhyles, their dying to delay,
Thou doest emmarble the proud hart of her
Whose love before their life they doe prefer.   140

So hast thou often done (ay me, the more!)
To me thy vassall, whose yet bleeding hart
With thousand wounds thou mangled hast so sore,
That whole remaines scarse any little part;
Yet, to augment the anguish of my smart,
Thou hast enfrosen her disdainefull brest,
That no one drop of pitie there doth rest.

Why then do I this honor unto thee,
Thus to ennoble thy victorious name,
Since thou doest shew no favour unto mee,   150
Ne once move ruth in that rebellious Dame,
Somewhat to slacke the rigour of my flame?
Certes small glory doest thou winne hereby,
To let her live thus free, and me to dy.

But if thou be indeede, as men thee call,
The worlds great Parent, the most kind preserver
Of living wights, the soveraine Lord of all,
How falles it then that with thy furious fervour
Thou doest afflict as well the not-deserver,
As him that doeth thy lovely heasts despize, 160
And on thy subjects most doest tyrannize?

Yet herein eke thy glory seemeth more,
By so hard handling those which best thee serve,
That, ere thou doest them unto grace restore,
Thou mayest well trie if they will ever swerve,
And mayest them make it better to deserve,
And, having got it, may it more esteeme;
For things hard gotten men more dearely deeme.

So hard those heavenly beauties he enfyred
As things divine, least passions doe impresse, 170
The more of stedfast mynds to be admyred,
The more they stayed be on stedfastnesse;
But baseborne mynds such lamps regard the lesse,
Which at first blowing take not hastie fyre;
Such fancies feele no love, but loose desyre.

For love is Lord of truth and loialtie,
Lifting himselfe out of the lowly dust
On golden plumes up to the purest skie,
Above the reach of loathly sinfull lust,
Whose base affect through cowardly distrust 180
Of his weake wings dare not to heaven fly,
But like a moldwarpe in the earth doth ly.

His dunghill thoughts, which do themselves enure
To dirtie drosse, no higher dare aspyre,
Ne can his feeble earthly eyes endure

The flaming light of that celestiall fyre
Which kindleth love in generous desyre,
And makes him mount above the native might
Of heavie earth, up to the heavens hight.

Such is the powre of that sweet passion,   190
That it all sordid basenesse doth expell,
And the refyned mynd doth newly fashion
Unto a fairer forme, which now doth dwell
In his high thought, that would it selfe excell,
Which he beholding still with constant sight,
Admires the mirrour of so heavenly light.

Whose image printing in his deepest wit,
He thereon feeds his hungrie fantasy,
Still full, yet never satisfyde with it;
Like Tantale, that in store doth sterved ly,   200
So doth he pine in most satiety;
For nought may quench his infinite desyre,
Once kindled through that first conceived fyre.

Thereon his mynd affixed wholly is,
Ne thinks on ought but how it to attaine;
His care, his joy, his hope, is all on this,
That seemes in it all blisses to containe,
In sight whereof all other blisse seemes vaine:
Thrise happie man! might he the same possesse,
He faines himselfe, and doth his fortune blesse.   210

And though he do not win his wish to end,
Yet thus farre happie he himselfe doth weene,
That heavens such happie grace did to him lend,
As thing on earth so heavenly to have seene
His harts enshrined saint, his heavens queene,
Fairer then fairest, in his fayning eye,
Whose sole aspect he counts felicitye.

Then forth he casts in his unquiet thought,
What he may do, her favour to obtaine;
What brave exploit, what perill hardly wrought   220
What puissant conquest, what adventurous paine,
May please her best, and grace unto him gaine;
He dreads no danger, nor misfortune feares,
His faith, his fortune, in his breast he beares.

Thou art his god, thou art his mightie guyde,
Thou, being blind, letst him not see his feares,
But cariest him to that which he hath eyde,
Through seas, through flames, through thousand swords
          and speares;
Ne ought so strong that may his force withstand,
With which thou armest his resistlesse hand.   230

Witnesse Leander in the Euxine waves,
And stout Æneas in the Trojane fyre,
Achilles preassing through the Phrygian glaives,
And Orpheus, daring to provoke the yre
Of damned fiends, to get his love retyre;
For both through heaven and hell thou makest way
To win them worship which to thee obay.

And if, by all these perils and these paynes,
He may but purchase lyking in her eye,
What heavens of joy then to himselfe he faynes!   240
Eftsoones he wypes quite out of memory
Whatever ill before he did aby:
Had it bene death, yet would he die againe,
To live thus happie as her grace to gaine.

Yet, when he hath found favour to his will,
He nathëmore can so contented rest,
But forceth further on, and striveth still

T' approch more neare, till in her inmost brest
He may embosomd bee and loved best;
And yet not best, but to be lov'd alone;   250
For love can not endure a Paragone.

The feare whereof, O how doth it torment
His troubled mynd with more then hellish paine!
And to his fayning fansie represent
Sights never seene, and thousand shadowes vaine,
To breake his sleepe, and waste his ydle braine:
Thou that hast never lov'd canst not beleeve
Least part of th' evils which poore lovers greeve.

The gnawing envie, the hart-fretting feare,
The vaine surmizes, the distrustfull showes,   260
The false reports that flying tales doe beare,
The doubts, the daungers, the delayes, the woes,
The fayned friends, the unassured foes,
With thousands more then any tongue can tell,
Doe make a lovers life a wretches hell.

Yet is there one more cursed then they all,
That cancker-worme, that monster, Gelosie,
Which eates the hart and feedes upon the gall,
Turning all loves delight to miserie,
Through feare of loosing his felicitie.   270
Ah, Gods! that ever ye that monster placed
In gentle love, that all his joyes defaced!

By these, O Love! thou doest thy entrance make
Unto thy heaven, and doest the more endeere
Thy pleasures unto those which them partake,
As after stormes, when clouds begin to cleare,
The Sunne more bright and glorious doth appeare;
So thou thy folke, through paines of Purgatorie
Dost beare unto thy blisse, and heavens glorie.

There thou them placest in a Paradize   280
Of all delight and joyous happie rest,
Where they doe feede on Nectar heavenly-wize,
With Hercules and Hebe, and the rest
Of Venus dearlings, through her bountie blest;
And lie like Gods in yvorie beds arayd,
With rose and lillies over them displayd.

There with thy daughter Pleasure they doe play
Their hurtlesse sports, without rebuke or blame,
And in her snowy bosome boldly lay
Their quiet heads, devoyd of guilty shame,   290
After full joyance of their gentle game;
Then her they crowne their Goddesse and their Queene,
And decke with floures thy altars well beseene.

Ay me! deare Lord! that ever I might hope,
For all the paines and woes that I endure,
To come at length unto the wished scope
Of my desire, or might myselfe assure
That happie port for ever to recure!
Then would I thinke these paines no paines at all,
And all my woes to be but penance small.   300

Then would I sing of thine immortall praise
An heavenly Hymne, such as the Angels sing,
And thy triumphant name then would I raise
Bove all the gods, thee onely honoring
My guide, my God, my victor, and my king:
Till then, dread Lord! vouchsafe to take of me
This simple song, thus fram'd in praise of thee.

AN HYMNE IN HONOUR OF BEAUTIE.

Ah! whither, Love! wilt thou now carrie mee?
What wontlesse fury dost thou now inspire
Into my feeble breast, too full of thee?
Whylest seeking to aslake thy raging fyre,
Thou in me kindlest much more great desyre,
And up aloft above my strength doest rayse
The wondrous matter of my fyre to prayse.

That as I earst, in praise of thine owne name,
So now in honour of thy Mother deare,
An honourable Hymne I eke should frame,   10
And, with the brightnesse of her beautie cleare,
The ravisht harts of gazefull men might reare
To admiration of that heavenly light,
From whence proceeds such soule-enchaunting might.

Therto do thou, great Goddesse! Queene of Beauty,
Mother of love, and of all worlds delight,
Without whose soverayne grace and kindly dewty
Nothing on earth seemes fayre to fleshly sight,
Doe thou vouchsafe with thy love-kindling light
T' illuminate my dim and dulled eyne,   20
And beautifie this sacred hymne of thyne:

That both to thee, to whom I meane it most,
And eke to her, whose faire immortall beame
Hath darted fyre into my feeble ghost,
That now it wasted is with woes extreame,
It may so please, that she at length will streame
Some deaw of grace into my withered hart,
After long sorrow and consuming smart.

WHAT TIME THIS WORLDS GREAT WORK-MAISTER DID CAST
To make al things such as we now behold,   30
It seemes that he before his eyes had plast
A goodly Paterne, to whose perfect mould
He fashiond them as comely as he could,
That now so faire and seemely they appeare,
As nought may be amended any wheare.

That wondrous Paterne, wheresoere it bee,
Whether in earth layd up in secret store,
Or else in heaven, that no man may it see
With sinfull eyes, for feare it to deflore,
Is perfect Beautie, which all men adore;   40
Whose face and feature doth so much excell
All mortall sence, that none the same may tell.

Thereof as every earthly thing partakes
Or more or lesse, by influence divine,
So it more faire accordingly it makes,
And the grosse matter of this earthly myne
Which clotheth it thereafter doth refyne,
Doing away the drosse which dims the light
Of that faire beame which therein is empight.

For, through infusion of celestiall powre,   50
The duller earth it quickneth with delight,
And life-full spirits privily doth powre
Through all the parts, that to the lookers sight
They seeme to please; That is thy soveraine might,
O Cyprian Queene! which flowing from the beame
Of thy bright starre, thou into them doest streame.

That is the thing which giveth pleasant grace
To all things faire, that kindleth lively fyre,
Light of thy lampe; which, shyning in the face,

Thence to the soule darts amorous desyre,   60
And robs the harts of those which it admyre;
Therewith thou pointest thy Sons poysned arrow,
That wounds the life, and wastes the inmost marrow.

How vainely then doe ydle wits invent,
That beautie is nought else but mixture made
Of colours faire, and goodly temp'rament
Of pure complexions, that shall quickly fade
And passe away, like to a sommers shade;
Or that it is but comely composition
Of parts well measurd, with meet disposition!   70

Hath white and red in it such wondrous powre,
That it can pierce through th' eyes unto the hart,
And therein stirre such rage and restlesse stowre,
As nought but death can stint his dolours smart?
Or can proportion of the outward part
Move such affection in the inward mynd,
That it can rob both sense, and reason blynd?

Why doe not then the blossomes of the field,
Which are arayd with much more orient hew,
And to the sense most daintie odours yield,   80
Worke like impression in the lookers vew?
Or why doe not faire pictures like powre shew,
In which oft-times we nature see of art
Exceld, in perfect limming every part?

But ah! beleeve me there is more then so,
That workes such wonders in the minds of men;
I, that have often prov'd, too well it know,
And who so list the like assayes to ken,
Shall find by tryall, and confesse it then,
That Beautie is not, as fond men misdeeme,   90
An outward shew of things that onely seeme.

For that same goodly hew of white and red,
With which the cheekes are sprinckled, shal decay,
And those sweete rosy leaves, so fairely spred
Upon the lips, shall fade and fall away
To that they were, even to corrupted clay:
That golden wyre, those sparckling stars so bright,
Shall turne to dust, and loose their goodly light.

But that faire lampe, from whose celestiall ray
That light proceedes, which kindleth lovers fire,   100
Shall never be extinguisht nor decay;
But, when the vitall spirits doe expyre,
Unto her native planet shall retyre;
For it is heavenly borne and can not die,
Being a parcell of the purest skie.

For when the soule, the which derived was,
At first, out of that great immortall Spright,
By whom all live to love, whilome did pas
Downe from the top of purest heavens hight
To be embodied here, it then tooke light   110
And lively spirits from that fayrest starre
Which lights the world forth from his firie carre.

Which powre retayning still or more or lesse,
When she in fleshly seede is eft enraced,
Through every part she doth the same impresse,
According as the heavens have her graced,
And frames her house, in which she will be placed,
Fit for her selfe, adorning it with spoyle
Of th' heavenly riches which she robd erewhyle.

Therof it comes that these faire soules, which have   120
The most resemblance of that heavenly light,
Frame to themselves most beautifull and brave

Their fleshly bowre, most fit for their delight,
And the grosse matter by a soveraine might
Tempers so trim, that it may well be seene
A pallace fit for such a virgin Queene.

So every spirit, as it is most pure,
And hath in it the more of heavenly light,
So it the fairer bodie doth procure
To habit in, and it more fairely dight   130
With chearefull grace and amiable sight;
For of the soule the bodie forme doth take;
For soule is forme, and doth the bodie make.

Therefore where-ever that thou doest behold
A comely corpse, with beautie faire endewed,
Know this for certaine, that the same doth hold
A beauteous soule, with faire conditions thewed,
Fit to receive the seede of vertue strewed;
For all that faire is, is by nature good;
That is a signe to know the gentle blood.   140

Yet oft it falles that many a gentle mynd
Dwels in deformed tabernacle drownd,
Either by chaunce, against the course of kynd,
Or through unaptnesse in the substance fownd,
Which it assumed of some stubborne grownd,
That will not yield unto her formes direction,
But is deform'd with some foule imperfection.

And oft it falles, (aye me, the more to rew!)
That goodly beautie, albe heavenly borne,
Is foule abusd, and that celestiall hew,   150
Which doth the world with her delight adorne,
Made but the bait of sinne, and sinners scorne,
Whilest every one doth seeke and sew to have it.
But every one doth seeke but to deprave it.

Yet nathëmore is that faire beauties blame,
But theirs that do abuse it unto ill:
Nothing so good, but that through guilty shame
May be corrupt, and wrested unto will;
Nathelesse the soule is faire and beauteous still,
How ever fleshes fault it filthy make;   160
For things immortall no corruption take.

But ye, faire Dames! the worlds deare ornaments
And lively images of heavens light,
Let not your beames with such disparagements
Be dimd, and your bright glorie darkned quight;
But, mindfull still of your first countries sight,
Doe still preserve your first informed grace,
Whose shadow yet shynes in your beauteous face.

Loath that foule blot, that hellish fiërbrand,
Disloiall lust faire beauties foulest blame,   170
That base affections, which your eares would bland
Commend to you by loves abused name,
But is indeede the bondslave of defame;
Which will the garland of your glorie marre,
And quench the light of your bright shyning starre.

But gentle Love, that loiall is and trew,
Will more illumine your resplendent ray,
And adde more brightnesse to your goodly hew,
From light of his pure fire; which, by like way
Kindled of yours, your likenesse doth display;   180
Like as two mirrours, by opposd reflexion,
Doe both expresse the faces first impression.

Therefore, to make your beautie more appeare,
It you behoves to love, and forth to lay
That heavenly riches which in you ye beare,
That men the more admyre their fountaine may;

W.   2

For else what booteth that celestiall ray,
If it in darknesse be enshrined ever,
That it of loving eyes be vewed never?

But, in your choice of Loves, this well advize,   190
That likest to your selves ye them select,
The which your forms first sourse may sympathize,
And with like beauties parts be inly deckt;
For, if you loosely love without respect,
It is no love, but a discordant warre,
Whose unlike parts amongst themselves do jarre.

For Love is a celestiall harmonie
Of likely harts composd of starres concent,
Which joyne together in sweete sympathie,
To worke ech others joy and true content,   200
Which they have harbourd since their first descent
Out of their heavenly bowres, where they did see
And know ech other here belov'd to bee.

Then wrong it were that any other twaine
Should in loves gentle band combyned bee
But those whom heaven did at first ordaine,
And made out of one mould the more t' agree;
For all, that like the beautie which they see,
Streight do not love; for Love is not so light
As streight to burne at first beholders sight.   210

But they, which love indeede, looke otherwise,
With pure regard and spotlesse true intent,
Drawing out of the object of their eyes
A more refyned forme, which they present
Unto their mind, voide of all blemishment;
Which it reducing to her first perfection,
Beholdeth free from fleshes frayle infection.

And then conforming it unto the light,
Which in it selfe it hath remaining still,
Of that first Sunne, yet sparckling in his sight,   220
Thereof he fashions in his higher skill
An heavenly beautie to his fancies will;
And, it embracing in his mind entyre,
The mirrour of his owne thought doth admyre.

Which seeing now so inly faire to be,
As outward it appeareth to the eye,
And with his spirits proportion to agree,
He thereon fixeth all his fantasie,
And fully setteth his felicitie;
Counting it fairer then it is indeede,   230
And yet indeede her fairenesse doth exceede.

For lovers eyes more sharply sighted bee
Then other mens, and in deare loves delight
See more then any other eyes can see,
Through mutuall receipt of beamës bright,
Which carrie privie message to the spright,
And to their eyes that inmost faire display,
As plaine as light discovers dawning day.

Therein they see, through amorous eye-glaunces,
Armies of Loves still flying too and fro,   240
Which dart at them their litle fierie launces;
Whom having wounded, backe againe they go,
Carrying compassion to their lovely foe;
Who, seeing her faire eyes so sharpe effect,
Cures all their sorrowes with one sweete aspect.

In which how many wonders doe they reede
To their conceipt, that others never see!
Now of her smiles, with which their soules they feede,
Like Gods with Nectar in their bankets free;

Now of her lookes, which like to Cordials bee;   250
But when her words embássade forth she sends,
Lord, how sweete musicke that unto them lends!

Sometimes upon her forhead they behold
A thousand Graces masking in delight;
Sometimes within her eye-lids they unfold
Ten thousand sweet belgards, which to their sight
Doe seeme like twinckling starres in frostie night;
But on her lips, like rosy buds in May,
So many millions of chaste pleasures play.

All those, O Cytherea! and thousands more   260
Thy handmaides be, which do on thee attend,
To decke thy beautie with their dainties store,
That may it more to mortall eyes commend,
And make it more admyr'd of foe and frend;
That in mens harts thou mayst thy throne enstall,
And spred thy lovely kingdome over-all.

Then Iö, tryumph! O great Beauties Queene,
Advance the banner of thy conquest hie,
That all this world, the which thy vassals beene,
May draw to thee, and with dew fëaltie   270
Adore the powre of thy great Majestie;
Singing this Hymne in honour of thy name,
Cempyld by me, which thy poore liegeman am!

In lieu whereof graunt, O great Soveraine!
That she, whose conquering beautie doth captive
My trembling hart in her eternall chaine,
One drop of grace at length will to me give,
That I her bounden thrall by her may live,
And this same life, which first fro me she reaved,
May owe to her, of whom I it receaved.   280

And you, faire Venus dearling, my deare dread!
Fresh flowre of grace, great Goddesse of my life,
When your faire eyes these fearefull lines shal read,
Deigne to let fall one drop of dew reliefe,
That may recure my harts long pyning griefe,
And shew what wondrous powre your beauty hath,
That can restore a damned wight from death.

AN HYMNE OF HEAVENLY LOVE.

LOVE, lift me up upon thy golden wings,
From this base world unto thy heavens hight,
Where I may see those admirable things
Which there thou workest by thy soveraine might,
Farre above feeble reach of earthly sight,
That I thereof an heavenly Hymne may sing
Unto the God of Love, high heavens king.

Many lewd layes (ah! woe is me the more!)
In praise of that mad fit which fooles call love,
I have in th' heat of youth made heretofore,   10
That in light wits did loose affection move;
But all those follies now I do reprove,
And turned have the tenor of my string,
The heavenly prayses of true love to sing.

And ye that wont with greedy vaine desire
To reade my fault, and, wondring at my flame,
To warme your selves at my wide sparckling fire,
Sith now that heat is quenched, quench my blame,
And in her ashes shrowd my dying shame;
For who my passed follies now pursewes,   20
Beginnes his owne, and my old fault renewes.

  BEFORE THIS WORLDS GREAT FRAME, in which al things
Are now containd, found any being-place,
Ere flitting Time could wag his eyas wings
About that mightie bound which doth embrace
The rolling Spheres, and parts their houres by space,
That High Eternall Powre, which now doth move
In all these things, mov'd in it selfe by love.

It lov'd it selfe, because it selfe was faire;
(For faire is lov'd;) and of it selfe begot,   30
Like to it selfe his eldest sonne and heire,
Eternall, pure, and voide of sinfull blot,
The firstling of his joy, in whom no jot
Of loves dislike or pride was to be found,
Whom he therefore with equall honour crownd.

With him he raignd, before all time prescribed,
In endlesse glorie and immortall might,
Together with that third from them derived,
Most wise, most holy, most almightie Spright!
Whose kingdomes throne no thought of earthly wight 40
Can comprehend, much lesse my trembling verse
With equall words can hope it to reherse.

Yet, O most blessed Spirit! pure lampe of light,
Eternall spring of grace and wisedome trew,
Vouchsafe to shed into my barren spright
Some little drop of thy celestiall dew,
That may my rymes with sweet infuse embrew,
And give me words equall unto my thought,
To tell the marveiles by thy mercie wrought.

Yet being pregnant still with powrefull grace,   50
And full of fruitfull love, that loves to get
Things like himselfe, and to enlarge his race,
His second brood, though not in powre so great,
Yet full of beautie, next he did beget
An infinite increase of Angels bright,
All glistring glorious in their Makers light.

To them the heavens illimitable hight
(Not this round heaven, which we from hence behold,
Adornd with thousand lamps of burning light,
And with ten thousand gemmes of shyning gold,)   60

He gave as their inheritance to hold,
That they might serve him in eternall blis,
And be partakers of those joyes of his.

There they in their trinall triplicities
About him wait, and on his will depend,
Either with nimble wings to cut the skies,
When he them on his messages doth send,
Or on his owne dread presence to attend,
Where they behold the glorie of his light,
And caroll Hymnes of love both day and night.   70

Both day, and night, is unto them all one;
For he his beames doth still to them extend,
That darknesse there appeareth never none;
Ne hath their day, ne hath their blisse, an end,
But there their termelesse time in pleasure spend;
Ne ever should their happinesse decay,
Had not they dar'd their Lord to disobay.

But pride, impatient of long resting peace,
Did puffe them up with greedy bold ambition,
That they gan cast their state how to increase   80
Above the fortune of their first condition,
And sit in Gods owne seat without commission;
The brightest Angell, even the Child of Light,
Drew millions more against their God to fight.

Th' Almighty, seeing their so bold assay,
Kindled the flame of His consuming yre,
And with His onely breath them blew away
From heavens hight, to which they did aspyre,
To deepest hell, and lake of damned fyre,
Where they in darknesse and dread horror dwell,   90
Hating the happie light from which they fell.

So that next off-spring of the Makers love,
Next to Himselfe in glorious degree,
Degendering to hate, fell from above
Through pride, (for pride and love may ill agree)
And now of sinne to all ensample bee:
How then can sinfull flesh itselfe assure,
Sith purest Angels fell to be impure?

But that Eternall Fount of love and grace,
Still flowing forth His goodnesse unto all,   100
Now seeing left a waste and emptie place
In His wyde Pallace, through those Angels fall,
Cast to supply the same, and to enstall
A new unknowen Colony therein,
Whose root from earths base groundworke shold begin.

Therefore of clay, base, vile, and next to nought,
Yet form'd by wondrous skill, and by His might,
According to an heavenly patterne wrought,
Which He had fashiond in his wise foresight,
He man did make, and breathd a living spright   110
Into his face most beautifull and fayre,
Endewd with wisedomes riches, heavenly, rare.

Such He him made, that he resemble might
Himselfe, as mortall thing immortall could;
Him to be Lord of every living wight
He made by love out of His owne like mould,
In whom He might His mightie selfe behould;
For Love doth love the thing belov'd to see,
That like itselfe in lovely shape may bee.

But man, forgetfull of his Makers grace   120
No lesse then Angels whom he did ensew,
Fell from the hope of promist heavenly place,
Into the mouth of death, to sinners dew,

And all his off-spring into thraldome threw,
Where they for ever should in bonds remaine
Of never-dead yet ever-dying paine;

Till that great Lord of Love, which him at first
Made of meere love, and after liked well,
Seeing him lie like creature long accurst
In that deepe horror of despeyred hell,   130
Him, wretch, in doole would let no lenger dwell,
But cast out of that bondage to redeeme,
And pay the price, all were his debt extreeme.

Out of the bosome of eternall blisse,
In which he reigned with his glorious syre,
He downe descended, like a most demisse
And abject thrall, in fleshes fraile attyre,
That He for him might pay sinnes deadly hyre,
And him restore unto that happie state
In which he stood before his haplesse fate.   140

In flesh at first the guilt committed was,
Therefore in flesh it must be satisfyde;
Nor spirit, nor Angell, though they man surpas,
Could make amends to God for mans misguyde,
But onely man himselfe, who selfe did slyde:
So, taking flesh of sacred virgins wombe,
For mans deare sake he did a man become.

And that most blessed bodie, which was borne
Without all blemish or reprochfull blame,
He freely gave to be both rent and torne   150
Of cruell hands, who with despightfull shame
Revyling him, that them most vile became,
At length him nayled on a gallow-tree,
And slew the Just by most unjust decree.

O huge and most unspeakable impression
Of loves deepe wound, that pierst the piteous hart
Of that deare Lord with so entyre affection,
And, sharply launching every inner part,
Dolours of death into his soule did dart,
Doing him die that never it deserved,   160
To free his foes, that from his heast had swerved!

What hart can feele least touch of so sore launch,
Or thought can think the depth of so deare wound?
Whose bleeding sourse their streames yet never staunch
But stil do flow, and freshly still redound,
To heale the sores of sinfull soules unsound,
And clense the guilt of that infected cryme
Which was enrooted in all fleshly slyme.

O blessed Well of Love! O Floure of Grace!
O glorious Morning-Starre! O Lampe of Light!   170
Most lively image of thy Fathers face,
Eternall King of Glorie, Lord of Might,
Meeke Lambe of God, before all worlds behight,
How can we thee requite for all this good?
Or what can prize that thy most precious blood?

Yet nought thou ask'st in lieu of all this love,
But love of us, for guerdon of thy paine:
Ay me! what can us lesse then that behove?
Had he required life of us againe,
Had it beene wrong to aske his owne with gaine?   180
He gave us life, he it restored lost;
Then life were least, that us so litle cost.

But he our life hath left unto us free,
Free that was thrall, and blessed that was band;
Ne ought demaunds but that we loving bee,
As he himselfe hath lov'd us afore-hand,

And bound therto with an eternall band,
Him first to love that us so dearely bought,
And next our brethren, to his image wrought.

Him first to love great right and reason is,   190
Who first to us our life and being gave,
And after, when we fared had amisse,
Us wretches from the second death did save;
And last, the food of life, which now we have,
Even he himselfe, in his deare sacrament,
To feede our hungry soules, unto us lent.

Then next, to love our brethren, that were made
Of that selfe mould, and that selfe Makers hand,
That we, and to the same againe shall fade,
Where they shall have like heritage of land,   200
How ever here on higher steps we stand,
Which also were with selfe-same price redeemed
That we, how ever of us light esteemed.

And were they not, yet since that loving Lord
Commaunded us to love them for his sake,
Even for his sake, and for his sacred word,
Which in his last bequest he to us spake,
We should them love, and with their needs partake;
Knowing that, whatsoere to them we give,
We give to him by whom we all doe live.   210

Such mercy he by his most holy reede
Unto us taught, and to approve it trew,
Ensampled it by his most righteous deede,
Shewing us mercie (miserable crew!)
That we the like should to the wretches shew,
And love our brethren; thereby to approve
How much, himselfe that loved us, we love.

Then rouze thy selfe, O Earth! out of thy soyle,
In which thou wallowest like to filthy swyne,
And doest thy mynd in durty pleasures moyle,   220
Unmindfull of that dearest Lord of thyne;
Lift up to him thy heavie clouded eyne,
That thou his soveraine bountie mayst behold,
And read, through love, his mercies manifold.

Beginne from first, where he encradled was
In simple cratch, wrapt in a wad of hay,
Betweene the toylefull Oxe and humble Asse,
And in what rags, and in how base aray,
The glory of our heavenly riches lay,
When him the silly Shepheards came to see,   230
Whom greatest Princes sought on lowest knee.

From thence reade on the storie of his life,
His humble carriage, his unfaulty wayes,
His cancred foes, his fights, his toyle, his strife,
His paines, his povertie, his sharpe assayes,
Through which he past his miserable dayes,
Offending none, and doing good to all,
Yet being malist both of great and small.

And looke at last, how of most wretched wights
He taken was, betrayd, and false accused;   240
How with most scornefull taunts, and fell despights,
He was revyld, disgrast, and foule abused;
How scourgd, how crownd, how buffeted, how brused;
And lastly, how twixt robbers crucifyde,
With bitter wounds through hands, through feet, and syde!

Then let thy flinty hart, that feeles no paine,
Empierced be with pittifull remorse,
And let thy bowels bleede in every vaine,
At sight of his most sacred heavenly corse,

So torne and mangled with malicious forse;   250
And let thy soule, whose sins his sorrows wrought,
Melt into teares, and grone in grieved thought.

With sence whereof, whilest so thy softened spirit
Is inly toucht, and humbled with meeke zeale
Through meditation of his endlesse merit,
Lift up thy mind to th' Author of thy weale,
And to his soveraine mercie doe appeale;
Learne him to love that loved thee so deare,
And in thy brest his blessed image beare.

With all thy hart, with all thy soule and mind,   260
Thou must him love, and his beheasts embrace;
All other loves, with which the world doth blind
Weake fancies, and stirre up affections base,
Thou must renounce and utterly displace,
And give thy selfe unto him full and free,
That full and freely gave himselfe to thee.

Then shalt thou feele thy spirit so possest,
And ravisht with devouring great desire
Of his deare selfe, that shall thy feeble brest
Inflame with love, and set thee all on fire   270
With burning zeale, through every part entire,
That in no earthly thing thou shalt delight,
But in his sweet and amiable sight.

Thenceforth all worlds desire will in thee dye,
And all earthes glorie, on which men do gaze,
Seeme durt and drosse in thy pure-sighted eye,
Compar'd to that celestiall beauties blaze,
Whose glorious beames all fleshly sense doth daze
With admiration of their passing light,
Blinding the eyes, and lumining the spright.   280

Then shall thy ravisht soule inspired bee
With heavenly thoughts farre above humane skil,
And thy bright radiant eyes shall plainely see
Th' Idee of his pure glorie present still
Before thy face, that all thy spirits shall fill
With sweete enragement of celestiall love,
Kindled through sight of those faire things above.

AN HYMNE OF HEAVENLY BEAUTIE.

RAPT with the rage of mine own ravisht thought,
Through contemplation of those goodly sights,
And glorious images in heaven wrought,
Whose wondrous beauty, breathing sweet delights
Do kindle love in high conceipted sprights;
I faine to tell the things that I behold,
But feele my wits to faile, and tongue to fold.

Vouchsafe then, O thou most Almightie Spright!
From whom all guifts of wit and knowledge flow,
To shed into my breast some sparkling light   10
Of thine eternall Truth, that I may show
Some litle beames to mortall eyes below
Of that immortall beautie, there with thee,
Which in my weake distraughted mynd I see;

That with the glorie of so goodly sight
The hearts of men, which fondly here admyre
Faire seeming shewes, and feed on vaine delight,
Transported with celestiall desyre
Of those faire formes, may lift themselves up hyer,
And learne to love, with zealous humble dewty,   20
Th' eternall fountaine of that heavenly beauty.

Beginning then below, with th' easie vew
Of this base world, subject to fleshly eye,
From thence to mount aloft, by order dew,
To contemplation of th' immortall sky;
Of the soare faulcon so I learne to fly,
That flags awhile her fluttering wings beneath,
Till she her selfe for stronger flight can breath.

Then looke, who list thy gazefull eyes to feed
With sight of that is faire, looke on the frame   30
Of this wyde universe, and therein reed
The endlesse kinds of creatures which by name
Thou canst not count, much lesse their natures aime;
All which are made with wondrous wise respect,
And all with admirable beautie deckt.

First, th' Earth, on adamantine pillers founded
Amid the Sea, engirt with brasen bands;
Then th' Aire still flitting, but yet firmely bounded
On everie side, with pyles of flaming brands,
Never consum'd, nor quencht with mortall hands;   40
And, last, that mightie shining christall wall,
Wherewith he hath encompassed this All.

By view whereof it plainly may appeare,
That still as every thing doth upward tend,
And further is from earth, so still more cleare
And faire it growes, till to his perfect end
Of purest beautie it at last ascend;
Ayre more then water, fire much more then ayre,
And heaven then fire, appeares more pure and fayre.

Looke thou no further, but affixe thine eye   50
On that bright shynie round still moving Masse,
The house of blessed God, which men call Skye,
All sowd with glistring stars more thicke then grasse,
Whereof each other doth in brightnesse passe,
But those two most, which, ruling night and day,
As King and Queene, the heavens Empire sway;

And tell me then, what hast thou ever seene
That to their beautie may compared bee,
Or can the sight that is most sharpe or keene
Endure their Captains flaming head to see?   60

w.   3

How much lesse those, much higher in degree,
And so much fairer, and much more then these,
As these are fairer then the land and seas?

For farre above these heavens, which here we see,
Be others farre exceeding these in light,
Not bounded, not corrupt, as these same bee,
But infinite in largenesse and in hight,
Unmoving, uncorrupt, and spotlesse bright,
That need no Sunne t' illuminate their spheres,
But their owne native light farre passing theirs.   70

And as these heavens still by degrees arize,
Untill they come to their first Movers bound,
That in his mightie compasse doth comprize,
And carrie all the rest with him around;
So those likewise doe by degrees redound,
And rise more faire, till they at last arive
To the most faire, whereto they all do strive.

Faire is the heaven where happy soules have place,
In full enjoyment of felicitie,
Whence they doe still behold the glorious face   80
Of the Divine Eternall Majestie;
More faire is that, where those Idees on hie
Enraunged be, which Plato so admyred,
And pure Intelligences from God inspyred.

Yet fairer is that heaven, in which doe raine
The soveraine Powres and mightie Potentates,
Which in their high protections doe containe
All mortall Princes and imperiall States;
And fayrer yet, whereas the royall Seates
And heavenly Dominations are set,   90
From whom all earthly governance is fet.

Yet farre more faire be those bright Cherubins,
Which all with golden wings are overdight,
And those eternall burning Seraphins,
Which from their faces dart out fierie light;
Yet fairer then they both, and much more bright,
Be th' Angels and Archangels, which attend
On Gods owne person, without rest or end.

These thus in faire each other farre excelling,
As to the Highest they approch more neare,   100
Yet is that Highest farre beyond all telling,
Fairer then all the rest which there appeare,
Though all their beauties joynd together were;
How then can mortall tongue hope to expresse
The image of such endlesse perfectnesse?

Cease then, my tongue! and lend unto my mynd
Leave to bethinke how great that beautie is,
Whose utmost parts so beautifull I fynd;
How much more those essentiall parts of his,
His truth, his love, his wisedome, and his blis,   110
His grace, his doome, his mercy, and his might,
By which he lends us of himselfe a sight!

Those unto all he daily doth display,
And shew himselfe in th' image of his grace,
As in a looking-glasse, through which he may
Be seene of all his creatures vile and base,
That are unable else to see his face,
His glorious face! which glistereth else so bright,
That th' Angels selves can not endure his sight.

But we, fraile wights! whose sight cannot sustaine   120
The Suns bright beames when he on us doth shyne,
But that their points rebutted backe againe
Are duld, how can we see with feeble eyne

The glory of that Majestie Divine,
In sight of whom both Sun and Moone are darke,
Compared to his least resplendent sparke?

The meanes, therefore, which unto us is lent
Him to behold, is on his workes to looke,
Which he hath made in beauty excellent,
And in the same, as in a brasen booke,   130
To reade enregistred in every nooke
His goodnesse, which his beautie doth declare;
For all thats good is beautifull and faire.

Thence gathering plumes of perfect speculation,
To impe the wings of thy high flying mynd,
Mount up aloft through heavenly contemplation,
From this darke world, whose damps the soule do blynd,
And, like the native brood of Eagles kynd,
On that bright Sunne of Glorie fixe thine eyes,
Clear'd from grosse mists of fraile infirmities.   140

Humbled with feare and awfull reverence,
Before the footestoole of his Majestie
Throw thy selfe downe, with trembling innocence,
Ne dare looke up with córruptible eye
On the dred face of that great Deity,
For feare, lest if he chaunce to looke on thee,
Thou turne to nought, and quite confounded be.

But lowly fall before his mercie seate,
Close covered with the Lambes integrity
From the just wrath of his avengefull threate   150
That sits upon the righteous throne on hy;
His throne is built upon Eternity,
More firme and durable then steele or brasse,
Or the hard diamond, which them both doth passe.

His scepter is the rod of Righteousnesse,
With which he bruseth all his foes to dust,
And the great Dragon strongly doth represse,
Under the rigour of his judgement just;
His seate is Truth, to which the faithfull trust,
From whence proceed her beames so pure and bright
That all about him sheddeth glorious light: 161

Light, farre exceeding that bright blazing sparke
Which darted is from Titans flaming head,
That with his beames enlumineth the darke
And dampish aire, whereby al things are red;
Whose nature yet so much is marvelled
Of mortall wits, that it doth much amaze
The greatest wisards which thereon do gaze.

But that immortall light, which there doth shine,
Is many thousand times more bright, more cleare,   170
More excellent, more glorious, more divine,
Through which to God all mortall actions here,
And even the thoughts of men, do plaine appeare;
For from th' Eternall Truth it doth proceed,
Through heavenly vertue which her beames doe breed.

With the great glorie of that wondrous light
His throne is all encompassed around,
And hid in his owne brightnesse from the sight
Of all that looke thereon with eyes unsound;
And underneath his feet are to be found   180
Thunder, and lightning, and tempestuous fyre,
The instruments of his avenging yre.

There in his bosome Sapience doth sit,
The soveraine dearling of the Deity,
Clad like a Queene in royall robes, most fit
For so great powre and peerelesse majesty,

And all with gemmes and jewels gorgeously
Adornd, that brighter then the starres appeare,
And make her native brightnes seem more cleare.

And on her head a crowne of purest gold   190
Is set, in signe of highest soveraignty;
And in her hand a scepter she doth hold,
With which she rules the house of God on hy,
And menageth the ever-moving sky,
And in the same these lower creatures all
Subjected to her powre imperiall.

Both heaven and earth obey unto her will,
And all the creatures which they both containe;
For of her fulnesse which the world doth fill
They all partake, and do in state remaine   200
As their great Maker did at first ordaine,
Through observation of her high beheast,
By which they first were made, and still increast.

The fairenesse of her face no tongue can tell;
For she the daughters of all wemens race,
And Angels eke, in beautie doth excell,
Sparkled on her from Gods owne glorious face,
And more increast by her owne goodly grace,
That it doth farre exceed all humane thought,
Ne can on earth compared be to ought.   21c

Ne could that Painter (had he lived yet)
Which pictured Venus with so curious quill,
That all posteritie admyred it,
Have purtrayd this, for all his maistring skill;
Ne she her selfe, had she remained still,
And were as faire as fabling wits do fayne,
Could once come neare this beauty soverayne.

But had those wits, the wonders of their dayes,
Or that sweete Teian Poet, which did spend
His plenteous vaine in setting forth her prayse,   220
Seene but a glims of this which I pretend,
How wondrously would he her face commend,
Above that Idole of his fayning thought,
That all the world shold with his rimes be fraught!

How then dare I, the novice of his Art,
Presume to picture so divine a wight,
Or hope t' expresse her least perfections part,
Whose beautie filles the heavens with her light,
And darkes the earth with shadow of her sight?
Ah, gentle Muse! thou art too weake and faint   230
The pourtraict of so heavenly hew to paint.

Let Angels, which her goodly face behold
And see at will, her soveraigne praises sing,
And those most sacred mysteries unfold
Of that faire love of mightie heavens King;
Enough is me t' admyre so heavenly thing,
And, being thus with her huge love possest,
In th' only wonder of her selfe to rest,

But who so may, thrise happie man him hold,
Of all on earth whom God so much doth grace,   240
And lets his owne Beloved to behold;
For in the view of her celestiall face
All joy, all blisse, all happinesse, have place;
Ne ought on earth can want unto the wight
Who of her selfe can win the wishfull sight.

For she, out of her secret threasury
Plentie of riches forth on him will powre,
Even heavenly riches, which there hidden ly
Within the closet of her chastest bowre,

Th' eternall portion of her precious dowre,   250
Which mighty God hath given to her free,
And to all those which thereof worthy bee.

None thereof worthy be, but those whom shee
Vouchsafeth to her presence to receave,
And letteth them her lovely face to see,
Whereof such wondrous pleasures they conceave,
And sweete contentment, that it doth bereave
Their soule of sense, through infinite delight,
And them transport from flesh into the spright.

In which they see such admirable things,   260
As carries them into an extasy,
And heare such heavenly notes and carolings,
Of Gods high praise, that filles the brasen sky;
And feele such joy and pleasure inwardly,
That maketh them all worldly cares forget,
And onely thinke on that before them set.

Ne from thenceforth doth any fleshly sense,
Or idle thought of earthly things, remaine;
But all that earst seemd sweet seemes now offense,
And all that pleased earst now seemes to paine;   270
Their joy, their comfort, their desire, their gaine,
Is fixed all on that which now they see;
All other sights but fayned shadowes bee.

And that faire lampe, which useth to inflame
The hearts of men with selfe-consuming fyre
Thenceforth seemes fowle, and full of sinfull blame;
And all that pompe to which proud minds aspyre
By name of honor, and so much desyre,
Seemes to them basenesse, and all riches drosse,
And all mirth sadnesse, and all lucre losse.   280

So full their eyes are of that glorious sight,
And senses fraught with such satietie,
That in nought else on earth they can delight,
But in th' aspect of that felicitie,
Which they have written in their inward ey;
On which they feed, and in their fastened mynd
All happie joy and full contentment fynd.

Ah, then, my hungry soule! which long hast fed
On idle fancies of thy foolish thought,
And, with false beauties flattring bait misled,   290
Hast after vaine deceiptfull shadowes sought,
Which all are fled, and now have left thee nought
But late repentance through thy follies prief;
Ah! ceasse to gaze on matter of thy grief:

And looke at last up to that Soveraine Light,
From whose pure beams al perfect beauty springs,
That kindleth love in every godly spright
Even the love of God; which loathing brings
Of this vile world and these gay-seeming things;
With whose sweete pleasures being so possest,   300
Thy straying thoughts henceforth for ever rest.

NOTES.

METRE OF THE FOUR HYMNS.

Spenser's Hymns are written in the seven lined stanza which was one of the favourite metres of Chaucer and is that characteristic of what is generally known as the 'Italian' period of his work in which the influence of Italian models is predominant. The seven lined stanza is really an adaptation of the Italian 'ottava rima' made by omitting the fifth rhyme: the scheme of rhymes in the 'ottava rima' is *ababbabcc*; the scheme of the seven lined stanza is *ababbcc*; in some ways it is a better form than the 'ottava rima' itself which tends to fall sharply into two parts; in the seven lined stanza the couplet at the end follows immediately on the preceding couplet which is in its turn closely connected with the early part of the stanza.

It is worthy of note that the seven lined stanza is the foundation for the lovely and complex stanza which Spenser invented for his use in *The Faerie Queene*.

HYMN I.

Analysis: Introduction (1—42). (The poet announces his own subjection to the power of love and wishes to placate that power by offering it praise; he fears that his force is impaired by the suffering he has borne and calls upon love to inspire him; he appeals to the Muses and Nymphs to acknowledge the power of love since they have often experienced it and calls upon the ladies who inspire love to also join the procession in his honour.)

The Introduction is somewhat weak and conventional; the poet describes his own submission to love in terms which are almost abject, and the idea hinted in ll. 29—42 seems to be that of a kind of pageant in honour of love, resembling perhaps the Masque of Cupid as described in the third book of *The Faerie Queene* (Canto xii.).

1—3. The love that "long since...subdude my poor captived heart " probably refers to Spenser's love for Rosalind, the heroine of *The Shepheards Calender*; the love that is "raging now " is most likely his new passion for the lady of the *Amoretti* who, later on, became his wife. There is a similar contrast between the old and the new love in *The Faerie Queene*. (Bk VI. Cantos vii. and x.)

3. **stowre** : Spenser uses this word in a great variety of senses. It

is in reality the same word as 'stir' and should mean 'tumult' or 'confusion.' The true meaning is quite appropriate here. Spenser also uses it in the sense of danger, passion or battle or even a paroxysm. Cf. *Faerie Queene* (III. iii. 50), *Shepheard's Calender*, Jan. l. 51 etc.

8. **the force of this new flame** : perhaps the same described in the *Sonnets*, his love for the Elizabeth whom he afterwards married.

11. **to areed** : 'to tell' or 'declare.' Also used in the sense of 'to appoint' or 'to command.' *F. Q.* Stanza 1:

"Me, all too meane, the sacred Muse areeds."

13. **mighty Victors** : such as Aeneas and Achilles referred to in ll. 232–3.

with wyde wounds embrewed : stained with blood.

14. **by thy cruell darts** : the conventional conception of Love as Cupid, the archer. Spenser very often contrasts the love inspired by Cupid, mere licentiousness, with the true and noble passion : thus in the account of Charissa in the House of Holiness :

"Full of great love, but Cupids wanton snare

As hell she hated."   (*F. Q.* I. x. 30.)

It is also the masque of Cupid which Britomart has to overthrow (*F. Q.* III. 12).

In these stanzas, however, Spenser makes no distinction.

17. **should faint** : subject in l. 15 'my wits.'

18. **my great god-hed** : the god whom I worship, *i.e.* 'love.'

The suffix is derived from the A.-S. 'had' and its truer form is 'hood,' but the oblique case 'hed' or 'hede' is often used in M. E. and Spenser, who employs so many M. E. forms, is fond of it.

23. **thy silver bowres and secret blisse** : these bowers are described at length in Bk IV. of *The Faerie Queene* (Canto x.) where Scudamour describes how he ventures into them to find Amoret.

24. **in Venus lap** : hardly consistent with the dignity of Love as described later.

28. **gentle furie** : 'furie' has the Latin sense of 'ardent desire'; the word corresponds also to the Platonic μανία as used in the *Phaedrus*.

32. **kindly smarts** : 'kindly' may have the usual meaning or may signify 'natural'; the latter sense is very frequent in Spenser who takes it from Chaucer. Cf.

"An heard of Bulles, whom kindly rage doth sting."

(*F. Q.* I. viii. 11.)

34. **to receive**: to hear.

your glorie: (*i.e.* Love).

43—91. (Love was born of Venus and begotten of Plenty and Penurie and is at once the eldest and the youngest of the gods. When the world was still buried in Chaos, Love, wakened by Necessity, aroused himself; he moved through Chaos, kindling by his own heat and he arranged the different elements in order. The elements, air and earth, and water and fire, were opposed to each other until Love tempered them; he appointed them their places and bound them in ·chains of adamant but in every living creature all four elements are united.)

The birth of Love, begotten of Plenty and Penury, is taken from the speech of Socrates in the *Symposium*.

Phaedrus states that Love is the eldest of the gods and Agathon that he is the youngest; Spenser (like Ficino) accepts him as being both. The account of love tempering the elements and harmonising them is taken in its original idea from the speech of Eryximachus in the *Symposium* but the interpretation of Love as being in this way the inspiring principle of creation is due to Ficino (see Introduction III.).

55, 56. **And yet a...Peares**: *Symposium* 195 ἔστι δὲ κάλλιστος ὢν τοιόσδε· πρῶτον μὲν νεώτατος θεῶν. Also *Symposium* 178 τὸ γὰρ ἐν τοῖς πρεσβύτατον εἶναι τὸν θεὸν τίμιον, ᾗ δ' ὅς, τεκμήριον δὲ τούτου.

See also Ficino, *Commentarium in Convivium* (V. 10): "Amorem illum quo creantur coelestes seniorem illis : eum vero quo creatori suo afficiuntur, dicimus juniorem....Igitur amor principium est et finis, deorum primus atque novissimus."

56. **Peares** should really mean 'equals,' but Spenser employs it here, as indeed it is used in common parlance, to mean 'lords.'

57, 58. **For ere this...crept**: *Symposium* 178 Ἡσιόδῳ δὲ καὶ Ἀκουσίλεως μετὰ τὸ Χάος δύο τούτῳ γενέσθαι, Γῆν τε καὶ Ἔρωτα.

Also Ficino (I. 3): "Quis igitur dubitavit, quin amor statim chaos sequatur, praecedatque mundum et deos omnes, qui mundi partibus distributi sunt?"

63. **Clotho**: one of the Parcae.

71—73. **Yet wanting light...ray**: Ficino (I. 3) "Quia amore in deum conversa, ipsius fulgore refulsit....chaos instar informis, lumen amat dum aspicit, irradiatur aspiciendo, radium accipiendo rerum coloribus figurisque formatur....amor chaos comitatur, obscura illuminat."

75. **The world, that...make**: Ficino (I. 3) "amor praecedit mundum."

76, 77. **Whose sundrie parts...ever**: Ficino (I. 3) " Et cum primo informis sit et chaos amore in mentem directa acceptis ab ea formis sit mundus."

77. **lyen**: Spenser's participle is quite correct according to the A.-S. form of the verb.

80. **oontrary**: accent on the second syllable.

83, 84. **Ayre hated earth...yre**: Ficino (III. 2) " Per hunc (*i.e.* amor) sydera lumen suum in elementa diffundunt. Per hunc ignis sui caloris communione aerem movet, aer aquam, aqua terram : ac versa vice terra ad se trahit aquam, haec aerem, ille ignem."

85—89. **He then them...chaines**: Ficino (III. 3) " Quamobrem omnes mundi partes, quid unius artificis omnia sunt, ejusdem machinae membra inter se in essendo et vivendo similia, mutua quadam charitate sibi invicem vinciuntur, ut merito dici possit amor nodus perpetuus et copula mundi partiumque ; et ejus immobile sustentaculum, ac firmum totius machinae fundamentum."

88. **raines**: kingdoms. Frequent in M. E.

89. **Adamantine**: here meaning unbreakable.

90. **every living wight**: creature or thing. In A.-S. ' wiht' means ' anything.' Spenser generally uses ' wight' as equivalent to person, 'fowle misshapen wights' (*F. Q.* II. xi. 8), but in this particular passage it certainly includes animals and may include plants as well.

Eryximachus says that when the elements of heat and cold, moist and dry are properly blent they bring health and plenty to men, animals and vegetables. *Symposium* 188 ἐπεὶ καὶ ἡ τῶν ὡρῶν τοῦ ἐνιαυτοῦ σύστασις μεστή ἐστιν ἀμφοτέρων τούτων, καὶ ἐπειδὰν μὲν πρὸς ἄλληλα τοῦ κοσμίου τύχῃ ἔρωτος ἃ νυνδὴ ἐγὼ ἔλεγον, τά τε θερμὰ καὶ τὰ ψυχρὰ καὶ ξηρὰ καὶ ὑγρά, καὶ ἁρμονίαν καὶ κρᾶσιν λάβῃ σώφρονα, ἥκει φέροντα εὐετηρίαν τε καὶ ὑγίειαν ἀνθρώποις καὶ τοῖς ἄλλοις ζῴοις τε καὶ φυτοῖς, καὶ οὐδὲν ἠδίκησεν.

92—119. (The world, having been created by the power of Love, is also maintained by it. Everything is still pervaded by its influence. All creatures are moved by the power of love to multiply their race, animals for lust only, but man for the sake of immortality. He has still in him some sparks of the divine fire and so desires to embrace that which is most divine, namely beauty.)

This is really a paraphrase of the speech of Socrates (see Introduction II.). Socrates, however, ascribes the desire for immortality to animals as well as man ; man differs in the *kind* of immortality achieved because his is of the mind and not of the race only.

92, 93. So ever since...beheast: Ficino (III. 2) "Secundum vero illud nostrae orationis membrum, quo amor effector omnium et servator est dictus, ita probatur."

95. this goodly cope: the firmament or sky.

99, 100. Thereby they all...kynd: Ficino (III. 2) "Cupiditas perfectionis proprie propagandae amor quidam est."

"Herbae quoque ac arbores cupidae sui seminis propagandi sui similia gignunt. Animalia quoque, bruta et homines ejusdem cupiditatis illecebris ad procreandum sobolem rapiuntur."

104, 105. Not for lusts...progenie: *Symposium* 208 ταύτῃ τῇ μηχανῇ, ἔφη, θνητὸν ἀθανασίας μετέχει, καὶ σῶμα καὶ τἆλλα πάντα· ἀδύνατον δὲ ἄλλῃ· μὴ οὖν θαύμαζε εἰ τὸ αὑτοῦ ἀποβλάστημα φύσει πᾶν τιμᾷ· ἀθανασίας γὰρ χάριν παντὶ αὕτη ἡ σπουδὴ καὶ ὁ ἔρως ἕπεται.

110—112. Therefore in choice...race: *Symposium* 209 ζητεῖ δὴ οἶμαι καὶ οὗτος περιιὼν τὸ καλὸν ἐν ᾧ ἂν γεννήσειεν· ἐν τῷ γὰρ αἰσχρῷ οὐδέποτε γεννήσει· τά τε οὖν σώματα τὰ καλὰ μᾶλλον ἢ τὰ αἰσχρὰ ἀσπάζεται ἅτε κυῶν.

106. deducted spright: spirit which is derived from God; 'deducted' is used exactly in the Latin sense. 'Spright' is with Spenser an alternative for 'spirit' and no less dignified.

108. enlumind: it is one of Spenser's peculiarities (imitated from M. E.) to make frequent use of the French 'en' or 'em' where his contemporaries would have preferred a Latin form of prefix.

114—116. nought more divine...beame: *Phaedrus* 250 νῦν δὲ κάλλος μόνον ταύτην ἔσχε μοῖραν, ὥστ᾽ ἐκφανέστατον εἶναι καὶ ἐρασμιώτατον.

120—161. (The darts of Love are received through the eyes but penetrate the whole body and cause distress and grief; lovers spend their time in lamenting and they see continually the image of their beloved. Love laughs at and scorns their complaints. The poet marvels at the extent of his own sufferings and marvels still more that he will consent to praise love who has not as yet brought him aid.)

The description of the woes of the lover is evidently taken in part from the *Phaedrus*. It also offers a close resemblance to the opening paragraphs of Bruno's *De gl' heroici furori*, though the passage in question is too long to quote. Bruno's picture of the sufferings of the lover is most vivid, he lays stress on what seems the incomprehensible nature of his pain but insists that, in spite of it, Love is the universal lord and preserver.

122. **with countenance coy**: Warton proposed to read 'from.'

124. **their**: *i.e.* 'the lovers.'

126. **carefull**: filled with care—a sense very frequent with Spenser.

129. **The daies they...grone**: *Phaedrus* 251 καὶ ἐμμανὴς οὖσα οὔτ νυκτὸς δύναται καθεύδειν οὔτε μεθ' ἡμέραν οὗ ἂν ᾖ μένειν.

137. **The whyles**: Spenser is here using an archaic form somewhat incorrectly; if the demonstrative is used it ought to be with the simple accusative 'the while'; 'whiles' is an adverb formed from the genitive; in the modern 'whilst' the 't' is drawn in after the 's.' Spenser uses the two forms indifferently.

139. **emmarble**: to make marble. See note on l. 108.

146. **enfrosen**: see note on l. 108.

151. **Ne**: 'nor,' an archaic form of the negative. See *F. Q.* I. i. 22:

"His forces faile, ne can no lenger fight."

159. **the not-deserver**: *i.e.* the lover who has deserved no harm at the hands of love.

160. **heasts**: A.-S. 'hǣs,' command.

162—217. (The poet seeks to understand why the true servants of love are so afflicted: it is to teach them to value love when they have once obtained it. The best love cannot be won in a moment and that which is easily moved is of a light and ignoble kind. The true love is a lofty emotion which exalts the soul; ignoble love knows nothing of such raptures. The true passion expels all baseness and re-fashions the whole mind into a nobler image. The lover thinks of nothing else but the image of his beloved and how to attain her; even the sight of her is happiness in itself.)

The contrast between the love which is easily wakened but ignoble and the noble love which requires winning is essentially the contrast made in the *Phaedrus*; thence comes also the image used for the inspiration of love (Introduction II.) and the account of the whole-hearted service of the lover.

162. **eke**: A.-S. 'ēac,' 'also' or 'likewise.'

168. **gotten**: the A.-S. verb was strong but its correct participle would be 'getten' or 'geten.'

169—72. The meaning is not easy, probably "It is hard to set on fire such heavenly beauties, for divine things do not easily feel passion but, in proportion to their own steadfastness, they are admired by those who have steadfast minds."

172—175 "Baseborn minds care nothing for the love which is hard to win and they themselves do not feel the true love but only base desire."

180. **affect**: imitation.

182. **moldwarpe**: a mole. The second part of the word comes from the A.-S. 'weorpan' to throw: the animal which throws or flings about the earth.

183. **do themselves enure**: have accustomed themselves.

190—196. Is explained by *Symposium* 252. The lover always desires that the beloved should have a soul resembling his favourite god, and endeavours to mould him to it, *i.e.* he makes an ideal image of his beloved upon which he always meditates.

200. **Like Tantale**: Spenser gives a description of Tantalus in his account of the Garden of Proserpina (*F. Q.* II. vii. 58):

"Deepe was he drenched to the upmost chin,
    Yet gaped still as coveting to drinke
    Of the cold liquor which he waded in;
    And stretching forth his hand did often thinke
    To reach the fruit which grew upon the brinke;
    But both the fruit from hand and flood from mouth,
    Did fly abacke, and made him vainely swincke;
    The whiles he sterv'd with hunger, and with drouth,
    He daily dyde, yet never throughly dyen couth."

in store doth sterved ly: starves in the midst of plenty.

209, 210. He would believe himself thrice happy if he could attain his desire and bless his fortune.

216. **his fayning eye**: probably his rejoicing eye: this sense of the word 'fayn' is common in A.-S. and M. E. A possible meaning is the eye which is always 'fayning' or 'depicting' the image of the beloved.

218—244. (The lover is willing to undergo any toils for the sake of his beloved; he dreads no danger if he may only win her favour and becomes irresistible by his inspiration. If his achievements win him her favour he is content.)

A very similar idea is found in the *Phaedrus* but the main authority for this passage is in the *Symposium* (the speech of Phaedrus). Achilles is quoted among the examples of noble lovers, but Orpheus is not mentioned, as with Spenser, for the sake of praise; on the contrary he is blamed; he did not dare like Alcestis to die for love but contrived how he might enter Hades alive, and therefore the gods punished him by showing him only an apparition of her whom he sought, and herself they would not give up. Achilles died for the sake of Patroclus and his fidelity was such that he died, not even to preserve his friend's love but to avenge him after he was dead, so the gods rewarded him above all others and sent him to the Islands of the Blest.

218. he casts: considers. See for the sentiment of this stanza *F. Q.* III. ii. 7.

220. hardly wrought: wrought or achieved with difficulty.

228. Through seas, through...speares: Spenser is speaking generally but he perhaps remembers his own Britomart who has to pass through the fire to deliver Amoret. (*F. Q.* III. xi. 22, 25).

229—230. Ne ought so...hand: *Symposium* 179 καὶ μαχόμενοί γ᾽ ἂν μετ᾽ ἀλλήλων οἱ τοιοῦτοι νικῷεν ἂν ὀλίγοι ὄντες ὡς ἔπος εἰπεῖν πάντας ἀνθρώπους.

231. Euxine waves: strictly speaking the Euxine was the Black Sea; it was, of course, across the Hellespont that Leander swam.

232. Æneas in the Trojane fyre: It was his father Anchises whom Æneas bore on his back out of Troy. The allusion is not strictly appropriate here, for it is an example of filial love, and not of the kind Spenser celebrates.

233. Achilles preassing through the Phrygian glaives: Achilles is counted among the lovers because of his devotion to Patroclus.

Phrygian: Trojan.

glaives: swords.

234. Orpheus: Spenser takes the legend of Orpheus, as was usually done, to show the extremest degree of lover's devotion. This, however, is not in accordance with Plato. (See above.)

235. retyre: a noun. 'To get for his love permission to return.'

237. worship: honour. A Chaucerian use of which Spenser is fond. Cp. *F. Q.* I. i. 3:

"To winne him worshippe, and her grace to have."

241. Eftsoones: a word of Spenser's own coinage from 'eft' a form of 'after' and 'soon': shortly or briefly.

242. aby or **abie:** to suffer. Cp. *F. Q.* II. viii. 28:

"His life for dew revenge should deare abye."

246—273. (It is not enough for the lover to win his lady's favour; he must be the only one and he cannot endure a rival. Of all his other troubles jealousy is the worst; a lover is always full of fears, but jealousy turns his whole life to bitterness. It is the worst evil to be found in life.)

It is not necessary to seek any original for this passage but Bruno (*De gl' heroici furori*) has a whole section devoted to the miseries of jealousy which he describes even more vigorously than Spenser. Jealousy is the daughter of envy and love, turning all the joys of her father into pain ; she is a minister of torment and an infernal fury, poisoning the sweets of love; she enters the heart through a thousand doors ; if she could be shut out love would be as delightful without her as the world without hate and without death.

> "O d' invidia et amor figlia si ria,
> Che le gioie del padre volgi in pene...
> Ministra di tormento Gelosia.
> Tisifone infernal, fetid' Arpia,
> Che l' altrui dolce rapi et avvelene....
> Pena, ch' entri nel cor per mille porte !
> Se si potesse á te chiuder l' entrata,
> Tant' il regno d' amor saria piu vago,
> Quant' il mondo senz' odio et senza morte."

Plato does not condescend to discuss jealousy at length in either of his erotic dialogues though the speech of Lysias, which is read by Phaedrus, describes a contemptible kind of jealousy in the ignoble lover. (*Phaedrus* 233.) Spenser, like Bruno, considers jealousy as a concomitant even of noble love and one of its sharpest misfortunes.

246. **nathëmore**: none the more or none the better: a characteristic Spenserian word. Cp. *F. Q.* I. ix. 25 :

> "Yet nathemore by his bold hartie speach."

251. **Paragone**: a rival or equal.

The female ancestors of Britomart have performed deeds 'in paragone of proudest men.' (*F. Q.* III. iii. 54.)

254. **to his fayning fansie**: 'fancy' is used in Spenser and Elizabethan writers generally as equivalent to 'imagination.'

256. **ydle braine**: because occupied with idle in the sense of useless things. Cp. *F. Q.* I. v. 8 :

> "Through widest ayre making his ydle way."

260. **distrustfull showes**: appearances that are not to be relied on.

261. **flying tales**: reports.

263. **the unassured foes**: those whom the lover suspects to be enemies but cannot be certain if they are.

266—272. Jealousy is embodied by Spenser in *The Faerie Queene* in

the person of Malbecco, husband of Hellenore, one of the grimmest
and most horrible of his conceptions. (*F. Q.* III. x. 59.) He takes
refuge in a cave.

> " Ne ever is he wont on ought to feed
> But todes and frogs, his pasture poysonous,
> Which in his cold complexion doe breed
> A filthy blood, or humour rancorous,
> Matter of doubt and dread suspitious,
> That doth with curelesse care consume the hart,
> Corrupts the stomacke with gall vitious...
> And doth transfixe the soule with deathes eternall dart."

271—307. (It is by such paines and penalties as these that Love
enters into his heaven the delights of which are the more endeared to
him for all he has endured. Love places his servants in a Paradise,
full of pleasure and devoid of guilt or shame. The poet concludes by
hoping that he will be among these fortunate ones and promising, if he
is, to sing yet more exalted praises of love.)

This is a somewhat feeble termination for the hymn. There is a
description of the joys of happy lovers given in the *Phaedrus*, but it is
a much more noble one than Spenser's; if the better elements of the
mind prevail the lovers will pass their lives in happiness, enslaving
what is vicious in their souls and setting free what is noble, so they
will conquer in one of the three Olympian victories, nor can either
human wisdom or divine inspiration give more to man. *Phaedrus* 256

ἐὰν μὲν δὴ οὖν εἰς τεταγμένην τε δίαιταν καὶ φιλοσοφίαν νικήσῃ τὰ βελτίω
τῆς διανοίας ἀγαγόντα, μακάριον μὲν καὶ ὁμονοητικὸν τὸν ἐνθάδε βίον διά-
γουσιν, ἐγκρατεῖς αὐτῶν καὶ κόσμιοι ὄντες, δουλωσάμενοι μὲν ᾧ κακία
ψυχῆς ἐνεγίγνετο, ἐλευθερώσαντες δὲ ᾧ ἀρετή· τελευτήσαντες δὲ δὴ
ὑπόπτεροι καὶ ἐλαφροὶ γεγονότες τῶν τριῶν παλαισμάτων τῶν ὡς ἀληθῶς
Ὀλυμπιακῶν ἓν νενικήκασιν, οὗ μεῖζον ἀγαθὸν οὔτε σωφροσύνη ἀνθρωπίνη
οὔτε θεία μανία δυνατὴ πορίσαι ἀνθρώπῳ.

Spenser's conception does not develope so noble a harmony as this.

278. **thy folke**: thy people. The word contains a sense of
familiarity in Modern English which it did not possess in Anglo Saxon
and Middle English.

280. **There thou them placest in a Paradize.** This Paradise is
described at length by Scudamour in Bk IV. of *The Faerie Queene*
(Canto X.) for he visits it in order to obtain Amoret.

282. **heavenly-wize**: in the manner of the gods.

283. **Hercules and Hebe**: is mentioned as one of the ' dearlings ' of

Venus without doubt because of his susceptibility to love. It was
indirectly through his love for Iole that he met his death. After his
deification he became the husband of Hebe.

287. **thy daughter Pleasure** : *i.e.* the daughter of Love.

293. Pleasure is crowned their Goddess, but it is Love's altars which
they deck with flowers. In Scudamour's narrative it is the altar of
Venus on which sacrifices are made. The whole description somewhat
resembles that of Acrasia's bower.

296. **the wished scope** : the utmost extent of his wishes.

298. **to recure** : to recover or regain.

HYMN II.

Analysis: Introduction (1—28). (The poet, having praised Love,
is now led on to praise Aphrodite or Venus, the mother of Love. He
beseeches her to inspire him in his praise of herself and, above all, to
aid him in winning his lady.)

2. **wontlesse**: unaccustomed. The word comes from A.-S. 'wunian
and its literal meaning is to dwell. Frequent in Chaucer and Spenser.

4. **aslake** : slake or lessen.

7. **matter of my fyre** : that which causes my fire or passion, *i.e.*
beauty.

9. **thy Mother** : Aphrodite or Venus.

12. **gazefull** : the coining of such words is a typical feature of
Spenser's style.

16. **Mother of love, and of all worlds delight**: Cp. Lucretius:
"hominum divomque voluptas Alma Venus."

17. **kindly dewty** : natural power. The word is strained for the
sake of the rhyme.

20. **eyne** : A.-S. 'eagan'; the noun was weak and took a weak
plural. One of Spenser's many archaisms. Cp. *F. Q.* I. iv. 21 :
      "And eke with fatnesse swollen were his eyne."

22. **to thee** : Venus or beauty.

23. **to her** : the lady of the sonnets.

24. **ghost** : the A.-S. 'gāst' was used in the general meaning of
spirit and not limited to the spirit after death. Cp. *F. Q.* I. vii. 21 :
when Una wakens from her swoon :
    "Then gins her grieved ghost thus to lament and mourne."

29—63. (When the world was first created its Maker wrought it according to a wonderful pattern which he placed before his eyes; this pattern, wherever it may be, is perfect Beauty which is something far beyond the conception of man. All things which are beautiful upon earth are so according as they partake in greater or less degree of this perfect beauty. Its divine power is infused into matter and quickens and moulds it.)

The conception of the world being made by an artificer according to an eternal pattern and therefore fair and excellent is taken from Plato's *Timaeus*:

"The work of the artificer who looks always to the abiding and the unchangeable and who designs and fashions his work after an unchangeable pattern, must of necessity be made fair and perfect; but that of an artificer who looks to the created only and fashions his work after a created pattern, is not fair or perfect....

"Which of the patterns had the artificer in view when he made the world, the pattern which is unchangeable or that which is created? If the world be indeed fair and the artificer good, then, as is plain, he must have looked to that which is eternal.... Everyone will see that he must have looked to the eternal for the world is the fairest of creations and he is the best of causes."

The conception of the true Beauty, the idea of Beauty, being wholly beyond the power of man to grasp is found both in the *Phaedrus* and *Symposium*.

It is this beauty, Socrates explains in the *Symposium*, which, without any diminution or change in itself, is imparted to the changing beauties of all other things: (See Introduction II.)

29. What time: a phrase of which Spenser is very fond and which Milton copies from him: (*Lycidas*)

"What time the grey-fly winds her sultry horn."

Work-maister: Plato's δημιουργός or *Demiurge*.

38. Or else in heaven. In Hymn IV. Spenser definitely locates the Platonic 'ideas' in heaven.

40. perfect Beautie: the pattern already referred to, the idea of Beauty, Beauty in itself.

which all men adore: because according to Plato they have already seen it when they were inhabitants of a higher world and before they were imprisoned in the body. (*Phaedrus* 250.) Spenser does not explain how it is that all men adore this perfect beauty; he expressly states that they have never seen it on earth but he does not adopt the doctrine of pre-existence. Plato's argument is clear and logical enough; men love all manifestations of beauty because they *have* seen the eternal archetype and all earthly beauty reminds them of it but, in sacrificing the doctrine of reminiscence, Spenser has sacrificed the logical core of the argument.

41. **Whose face and feature**: appearance.

43, 44. **Thereof as every...divine.** Ficino explains that beauty is a spiritual thing, the splendour of God's light shining in all things.

"Pulchritudo actus quidam sive radius inde per omnia penetrans: Primo in angelicam mentem: Secundo in animam totius et reliquos animos: Tertio in naturam: Quarto in materiam corporum.... Materiam formis exornat." (II. v.)

46. **this earthly myne**: the earth is called a 'mine' either because it is low as compared with the heavenly world or because it provides material for the latter to work upon, probably both together.

49. **that faire beame**: beauty. Ficino's 'radius.'

empight: fixed within. The word is Chaucerian and has infinitive 'picchen' to fix.

51. **the duller earth**: Ficino's 'materia corporum.'

55. **Cyprian Queene**: Venus.

56. **thy bright starre**: possibly Beauty itself or Spenser may think that beauty is in some way due to the influence of the planet Venus. Ficino has a whole chapter concerning the influence of planets upon the forms and natures of men. (VI. 6.)

57—105. (It is this spirit or light which kindles beauty in all things and thus causes love. It is folly to say that beauty arises from nothing else but outward colours or the harmony of parts. What power have red and white in themselves that they can produce so great an effect or how is it that proportion can so tremendously influence the mind? In that case flowers and pictures would have as great an effect. The truth is that beauty is not an outward appearance only. All outward beauties can change and decay but the source from which they proceed cannot be extinguished, it is the soul itself and is a part of heaven.)

Spenser here follows Bruno and Ficino as closely as possible. (See Introduction III.)

59. **Light of thy lampe**: the lamp of Venus or Beauty.

64—66. **How vainely then...faire**: Bruno (p. 643) "Anzi quello che s' innamora del corpo é una certa spiritualitá che veggiamo in esso, la qual si chiama bellezza, la qual non consiste nelle dimensioni maggiori ò minori; non nelli determinati colori ò forme; ma in certa armonia."

68. And passe away, like to a sommers shade: Bruno (p. 672):
"la bellezza che si vede ne gli corpi é una cosa accidentale et umbratile."

69, 70. Or that it...disposition: Ficino (v. 3): "Sunt autem
nonnulli qui certam membrorum omnium positionem, sive, ut eorum
verbis utamur commensu rationem et proportionem, ut cum quadam
colorum suavitate, esse pulchritudinem opinentur."

73. stowre: distress or confusion.

79. orient hew: brilliant hue. 'Orient' really means eastern but
is often used in the other sense. Compare Carew's Song:

> "For in your beauty's orient deep
>
> These flowers, as in their causes, sleep."

82. Or why doe not faire pictures, etc. From Bruno.

84. The idea is that art may excel nature because a picture may
show every part in greater perfection than is possible in a living creature.

88. the like assayes to ken: to expose himself to similar trials.

ken: from the A.-S. 'cunnan.'

90. fond men: foolish.

90, 91. Beautie is not...seeme": Ficino (v. 3): "ipsa pulchritudo
spiritale quoddam potius rei simulacrum sit, quam corporea species."

92—98. All the outward appearance of the body will change.

Ficino (v. 3): "Siquidem corpus hominis unum atque idem hodie
formosum, cras autem casu aliquo foedante deforme: quasi aliud sit esse
corpus, aliud esse formosum."

So Bruno (p. 672): "Non certo, perche la non é vera ne constante
bellezza, et peró non può caggionar vero ne constante amore...il quale
sovente da bello si fá brutto senza che alteration veruna si faccia ne
l' anima."

95, 96. shall fade and...were: Bruno "che sono assorbite, alterate,
et guaste per la mutatione del suggetto."

99. that faire lampe: the soul which fills the body with beauty.

103. her native planet: Spenser accepted the Ptolemaic astronomy
which considered the sun as one of the planets and, as is shown by the
next verse, it must be the sun which is meant here.

105. a parcell—a small portion—the true sense of the word.

the purest skie: the heaven of heavens or empyrean. In Hymn IV.
Spenser explains how the heavens rise one above another, excelling in
' largenesse and in height' until they come

> "To the most faire, whereto they all do strive."

106—147. (When the soul passes down to earth it first takes life
and spirits from the sun. When it becomes embodied it retains this

power and transforms its corporal frame by means of it. Those souls
which are the noblest frame their bodies the most beautifully; the more
excellent the soul and the more lovely is the body; therefore a fair body
is witness of a fair soul. It often happens, however, that a fair soul
dwells in a body which is not beautiful because it has chanced upon
substance which is stubborn and imperfect.)

The underlying idea of this passage is taken directly from Ficino
and Bruno. (See Introduction III.)

107. **out of that great immortall Spright**: The Christian idea of
souls being derived from God. Plato supposes them to have existed
and even to have been upon earth before. (*Phaedrus* 248, 249.)

108. **whilome**: A.-S. 'hwilum.' In A.-S. the word means 'from time
to time' in Spenser 'formerly.'

109. **Downe from the top of purest heavens hight**: ὅταν δὲ δὴ
πρὸς δαῖτα καὶ ἐπὶ θοίνην ἴωσιν, ἄκραν ἐπὶ τὴν ὑπουράνιον ἁψῖδα πορεύ-
ονται πρὸς ἄναντες. (*Phaedrus* 247.)

Plato says that the souls which follow the gods come out upon the
summit of the heaven but it is only the strongest who can achieve
this.

112. **Which lights the world**, etc. The Egyptians and others
believed that the souls of men, before their embodiment upon earth,
came from the sun and brought with them a certain vital power. The
idea is common in the Neo-Platonists.

In Dante's *Paradiso* one of the heavens is placed in the sun.

113. **Which powre retayning**: the formative power derived from
the sun.

114. **eft**: afterwards.

enraced: embodied in the race of mortal men.

116—126. **According as the...Queene**: the more heavenly the soul
is and the more beautiful its body.

Compare Bruno (p. 672): "La raggion dumque apprende il piu vero
bello per conversione á quello che fá la beltade nel corpo, et viene á
formarlo bello, et questa é l' anima che l' há talmente fabricato et
infigurato."

Also Ficino (v. 6): "Harum vero fundamentum elementorum
quatuor temperata complexio, ut corpus nostrum coelo, cujus est
temperata substantia, sit simillimum neque aliquo humorum excessu
ab animi formatione desciscat. Sic enim coelestis fulgor facile lucebit
in corpore et forma hominis illa perfecta, quam habet animus in
pacatam obedientemque materiam resultabit expressior."

123. **bowre:** a dwelling place. The A.-S. 'būr,' used in an absolutely correct sense.

124. **And the grosse matter by a soveraine might:** Ficino (v. 3): "Quamvis enim corpora quaedam speciosa dicamus, non tamen sunt ex ipsa sui materia speciosa."

125. **Tempers so trim:** frames so excellently.

126. **a virgin Queene:** *i.e.* the soul. In *The Faerie Queene* (II. ix.) the Queen is described as Alma and the body as the House of Alma.

130. **more fairely dight:** arrange more beautifully. Cp. *F. Q.* I. iv. 6:

> "With rich array and costly arras dight."

132—133. **For of the...make:** Bruno (p. 647): "L' anima non é nel corpo localmente, ma come forma intrinseca, et formatore estrinseco; come quella che fá gli membri, et figura il composte da dentro et da fuori."

135. **corpse:** body. In Spenser's time the word frequently had its modern sense but not invariably.

137. **with faire conditions thewed:** endowed with fair qualities and manners; 'thewed' should not really be employed as a verb. In A.-S. it is a noun 'thēaw,' meaning virtue, and Spenser generally employs it in its correct sense.

There is, however, one parallel instance to the above (*F. Q.* II. vi. 26):

> "Yet would not seeme so rude, and thewed ill."

141—147. Ficino (VI. 6): "Saepenumero accidit, ut duo quidem animi licet diversis temporum intervallis, Jove tamen regnante descenderint! alterque illorum semen in terra nactus idoneum corpus secundum priores ideas illas rectissime figuraverit: alter vero propter materiae ineptitudinem, idem opus inchoaverit quadam, sed non tanta ad sui exemplar fuerit similitudine executus. Corpus illud isto formosius."

See also Ficino (v. 6): "Quid tandem est corporis pulchritudo? Actus vivacitas et gratia quaedam ideae suae influxu in ipso refulgens. Fulgor hujusmodi in materiam non prius quam aptissime sit praeparata descendit."

142. **tabernacle:** dwelling place.

143. **kynd:** nature—a Chaucerian word.

146. **her formes direction:** Cp. Bruno: "forma intrinseca et formatore estrinseco."

148—182. (The poet proceeds to contrast the two kinds of love. Beauty, though noble in itself, may be put to the basest of uses but that is not its blame but the blame of those who misuse it. The poet be-

seeches all fair ladies to maintain an inward beauty that shall correspond
to the outward one; they must loathe that lust which is the greatest
enemy of beauty and encourage only the love which is loyal and true.)

The general contrast between the two kinds of love comes from the
Symposium, the speech of Pausanius. The love which is of the body
rather than of the soul is essentially evil whereas the love of the noble
mind is lifelong.

Symposium 183 : πονηρὸς δ᾽ ἔστιν ἐκεῖνος ὁ ἐραστὴς ὁ πάνδημος, ὁ τοῦ
σώματος μᾶλλον ἢ τῆς ψυχῆς ἐρῶν· καὶ γὰρ οὐδὲ μόνιμός ἐστιν, ἅτε οὐδὲ
μονίμου ἐρῶν πράγματος· ἅμα γὰρ τῷ τοῦ σώματος ἄνθει λήγοντι, οὗπερ
ἤρα, οἴχεται ἀποπτάμενος, πολλοὺς λόγους καὶ ὑποσχέσεις καταισχύνας·
ὁ δὲ τοῦ ἤθους χρηστοῦ ὄντος ἐραστὴς διὰ βίου μένει, ἅτε μονίμῳ συντακείς.

150. **that celestiall hew**: 'hew' is the A.-S. 'hiw' and means the
whole outer appearance, not only the colour. *F. Q.* I. i. 46:

"Whose semblance she did carrie under feigned hew."

158. **unto will**: *i.e.* the will of the evil doer.

162. **the worlds deare ornaments**: Cp. *Sonnet* 74.

"my love, my life's last ornament."

166. **your first countries sight**: *i.e.* the things which they have
seen in heaven. *Phaedrus* 250, 251.

167. **your first informed grace**: the grace with which they were
first filled.

168. **whose shadow yet...face**: Bruno 643 "onde é che l' affetto
ben formato ama gli corpi ò la corporal bellezza, per quel che é indice
della bellezza del spirito."

169. **flër**: pronounced as a dissyllable very frequently both in
Spenser and Shakespeare.

171. **bland**: from 'blend,' meaning to confuse and bewilder.

181, 182. **Like as two...impression**. In the *Phaedrus* (255) the
lover is compared to a mirror in which the beloved beholds himself:
ὥσπερ δὲ ἐν κατόπτρῳ ἐν τῷ ἐρῶντι ἑαυτὸν ὁρῶν λέληθεν.

Also Ficino (II. 8): "Fit itaque amantis animus speculum in quo
amati relucet imago."

183—238. (The poet calls upon all ladies to win love by revealing
not only their beauty but also the heavenly riches of their minds. In
choosing a love they would be well advized to choose those who are
akin to them or whose souls originate from the same source. There
cannot be true harmony in love unless the lovers are born under har-
monious conjunctions of the stars and have been all along destined for

each other. No others should be wedded except those who are made
out of the same mould. True love cannot arise in a moment; the true
lover does not see only the outward form of his beloved, he perceives
the inner and more refined form, the true image of the soul, and beholds
it as if it were free from the imperfections of the body; this image he
sees continually in his own mind. This is why lovers always think their
beloved more beautiful than others do, and they are right, for others see
nothing but the outward form.)

The substance of this passage is taken directly from Ficino and
Bruno. Ficino explains at length, (vi. 6) and (ii. 8), how lovers are
born, either under the same planet or under an. apt conjunction of
stellar influences and both Ficino and Bruno explain how what the lover
sees is not really the outer form of the beloved but a creation of his
own mind which, nevertheless, is an expression of the inmost self of the
beloved. (See Introduction iii.)

192, 193. **The which your...deckt**: Ficino (vi. 6): "Quo fit ut
non formosissimos quoque sed suos, id est similiter natos etiam si minus
quam alii multi formosi sint, quilibet maxime diligant."

194. **without respect**: without consideration.

197, 198. **For Love is...concent.** Ficino (vi. 6): "Proinde qui, ut
diximus, eodem sunt astro sub orti, ita se habent, ut pulchrioris eorum
simulacrum, per oculos in alterius animum manans, consimili cuidam
simulachro, tam in corpore aethereo, quam in animi penetralibus ab ipsa
generatione formato quadret, et undique consonet."

See also Ficino (ii. 8): "Iccirco amatus cum in amante se recog-
noscat, amare illum compellitur. Vicissitudinem amoris inter illos
praecipuam esse astrologi arbitrantur, in quorum genesi luminum, id
est solis et lunae, commutatio fuerit. Videlicet si me nascente sol in
ariete, luna in libra. Te nascente sol in libra, luna in ariete. Aut
quibus signum idem simileve idemque planeta similisve ascenderit: aut
benigni planetae similiter angulum orientis aspexerint, aut Venus in
eadem nativitatis domo, eodemque gradu fuerit constituta."

208—215. **For all that...blemishment.** Bruno (p. 658): "Intendo
che non é la figura ó la specie sensibilmente ó intelligibilmente repre-
sentata, la quale per se muove: perche mentre alchuno stà mirando la
figura manifesta à gl' occhi, non viene anchora ad amare: ma da quello
instante, che l' animo concipe in se stesso quella figurata non piu visibile
ma cogitabile, non piu sotte specie di cosa, ma sotto specie di buono,
ó bello: all' hora subito nasce l' amore."

Also Ficino (VI. 6): "Animo igitur formosi hominis simulachrum conceptum semel apud se reformatum: memoriter conservanti satis esset amatum quandoque vidisse."

221—224. Thereof he fashions...admyre. Ficino (VI. 6): "si quod illi deest, at perfectam corporis Jovialis effigiem instaurat reformando: ipsum deinde reformatum simulacrum tanquam opus proprium deligit."

"Oculo tamen et spiritui, quae veluti specula praesente corpore imagines capiunt, absente dimittunt, perpetua formosi corporis praesentia opus est, ut ejus illustratione continue lucescant, foveantur et oblectentur."

228. his fantasie: thought or imagination.

229. And fully setteth his felicitie: see Ficino above.

230. Counting it fairer then it is indeede: Ficino (VI. 6): "Hinc accidit, ut amantes ita decipiantur: ut formosiorem quam sit, existiment."

Also Bruno (p. 646): "Il divo dumque e vivo oggetto, ch' ei dice, é la specie intelligible piu alta che egli s' habbia possuto formar della divinitá; et non é qualche corporal bellezza che gl' adombrasse il pensiero come appare in superficie del senso?"

236. privie message: secret message.

239—287. (Lovers see an endless number of charms in their beloved; they delight in her words, her looks and her smiles. The poet concludes with celebrating once again, the power of Beauty and imploring her aid to gain his lady's mercy; he appeals to the lady herself.)

241. litle fierie launces: the arrows of love.

244. so sharpe effect: the keen power of her eyes.

247. To their conceipt: in their own minds.

249. bankets: banquets.

251. her words embássade: the embassy of her words.

256. sweet belgards: beautiful looks (a French word).

Compare with these lines the description of Belphoebe (*F. Q.* II. iii. 25).

> "Upon her eyelids many graces sate,
>   Under the shadow of her even browes,
>   Working belgardes and amorous retrate."

257. Doe seeme like...night: A reminiscence of Chaucer who says of his Friar:

> "His eyën twinkled in his heed aryght
>   As doon the sterrës in the frosty nyght."

260. Cytherea: Venus.

262. with their dainties store: the store of their beauties.

266. **over-all**: everywhere.

269. **beene**: quite correctly employed. One of the A.-S. forms which correspond to the modern 'are.'

274. **in lieu whereof**: in return for which.

279, 280. **And this same...receaved.** "That she may give me back again the life which she took from me."

281. **my deare dread**: the lady of the sonnets. The reader should compare the lovely description of her in *The Faerie Queene* (VI. x. 12—28).

282. **Fresh flowre of grace**: cp. *F. Q.* VI. x. 27:
        "Another Grace she well deserves to be,
            In whom so many Graces gathered are."

283. **fearefull**: timid.

284. **dew reliefe**: relief that has been well earned.

HYMN III.

Introduction (1—21). (The poet invokes love to inspire him so that he may see heavenly things. He regrets the character of the works he wrote in his youth and turns now to the praises of the true or heavenly love. He calls on his former readers to peruse what he now writes and so earn him forgiveness for his early faults.)

1—5. The imagery of the *Phaedrus* (250): κάλλος δὲ τότ᾽ ἦν ἰδεῖν λαμπρόν, ὅτε σὺν εὐδαίμονι χορῷ μακαρίαν ὄψιν τε καὶ θέαν, ἑπόμενοι μετὰ μὲν Διὸς ἡμεῖς, ἄλλοι δὲ μετ᾽ ἄλλου θεῶν, εἶδόν τε καὶ ἐτελοῦντο τῶν τελετῶν ἣν θέμις λέγειν μακαριωτάτην, ἣν ὠργιάζομεν ὁλόκληροι μὲν αὐτοὶ ὄντες καὶ ἀπαθεῖς κακῶν, ὅσα ἡμᾶς ἐν ὑστέρῳ χρόνῳ ὑπέμενεν, ὁλόκληρα δὲ καὶ ἁπλᾶ καὶ ἀτρεμῆ καὶ εὐδαίμονα φάσματα μυούμενοί τε καὶ ἐποπτεύοντες ἐν αὐγῇ καθαρᾷ, καθαροὶ ὄντες καὶ ἀσήμαντοι τούτου, ὃ νῦν δὴ σῶμα περιφέροντες ὀνομάζομεν, ὀστρέου τρόπον δεδεσμευμένοι.

8. **many lewd layes**: none of Spenser's existing works deserve this description but it is possible he is referring to some poems or portions of poems which are lost.

9. **that mad fit which fooles call love**: Cp. the description in *Colin Clout's Come Home Again.* (See Introduction I.)

10. **in th' heat of youth**: Spenser's earliest original poem *The Shepheard's Calender*, was published at the age of twenty-seven but he had probably written much before.

11. **did loose affection move**: Spenser can hardly be referring to

the two former hymns as they stand but probably in some preceding shape.

16. **To reade my fault**: the licentious poems already referred to.

20. **now pursewes**: follows by reading.

22—77. (Before time or the world existed the Great Eternal Power moved in itself by love; it loved its own beauty and begot of itself the Son and derived from them both the Holy Spirit. Through the same love the angels were next created.)

The main idea of this comes from a blending of Plato and Christianity. Diotima, as reported in the *Symposium*, teaches that love is a desire of birth in beauty and that the highest love is a desire of birth in the absolute beauty. Christianity teaches that God is love. Spenser identifies God also with the absolute beauty of Plato and, by combining these two ideas, respresents God as enjoying his own beauty and thus bringing to birth things which are fair.

In the *Timaeus* also, Plato represents God as creating the world in goodness and, being free from jealousy, he desired that all things should be as like himself as they could be (*Timaeus* 29).

24. **Ere flitting Time...wings**: Cp. *Timaeus* "Time, then, was created with the heaven in order that, being produced together, they might be dissolved together if ever there should be any dissolution of them."

flitting: swiftly moving.

wag: to stir, cf. A.-S. 'wagian.' Spenser's use is quite correct.

eyas: newly fledged young. Cp. *F. Q.* I. xi. 34:

"Like Eyas hawke up mounts unto the skies."

25. **that mightie bound**: the outer firmament of the fixed stars within which the orbits of the planets are contained, and by degrees of which the planetary hours were measured.

34. **Of loves dislike or pride**: there was nothing in him love could dislike and there was no pride.

36. **before all time prescribed**: before any fixed time. Cp. the *Timaeus*: "For there were no days and nights and months and years before the heaven was created, but when he created the heaven he created them also."

39. **most almightie Spright**: Spright is exactly the same as 'spirit' in Spenser. See note on Hymn I. l. 106.

42. **With equall words**: words suitable to the task.

47. **with sweet infuse embrew**: fill my lines with a sweet infusion.

55. **An infinite increase**: a great multitude.

58. **this round heaven**: the firmament of the fixed stars, the ' mightie bound ' already referred to.

64. **in their trinall triplicities.** According to the schoolmen there were ten orders of angels created but one fell with Lucifer, leaving nine.

66—67. **Either with nimble...send**: Cp. *F. Q.* II. viii. 22:

"How oft do they their silver bowers leave,

To come to succour us that succour want !

How oft do they with golden pinions cleave

The flitting skyes, like flying Pursuivant...

And all for love and nothing for regard,

O ! why should heavenly God to men have such reward?'

75. **their termelesse time**: time without limit.

78—119. (The brightest of the angels, Lucifer, through pride revolts against God and draws millions more to fight with him. They are cast out of heaven and, in order to supply their place, God creates the race of man; he moulds him out of clay but makes him according to the divine image.)

This general account of the fall of the angels and of the creation of man to supply their place is the same as that given afterwards by Milton in *Paradise Lost* (Bks VI. and VII.). Both Spenser and Milton take it from scholastic theology.

78. **But pride, impatient of long resting peace**: Cp. Wolsey in *Henry VIII.*:

"By that sin fell the angels."

82. **without commission**: without the right of doing so.

85. **seeing their so bold assay**: their bold attempt.

87. **with His onely breath**: needing nothing more than His breath.

This is not like Milton who represents them as assailed by all the host of heaven and then driven over the battlements by the lightnings of the Son.

91. **Hating the happie light from which they fell.** A very Miltonic line.

98. **Sith**: since. A.-S. 'siththan.'

100. **flowing forth**: ' flowing' is here made a transitive verb.

103. **Cast to supply**: planned to supply.

108. **According to an heavenly patterne wrought.** In the *Timaeus*, Plato describes God as making all things according to

a heavenly archetype or pattern but he does not explain how this ideal is derived, Plato cannot tell its origin and his Demiurge works like a human artificer though with infinitely greater power. Spenser, according to Christian teaching, concentrates all power in God and therefore makes God himself the author of the divine idea which he moulds first 'in his wise foresight' and makes the world according to it.

113, 114. **Such He him...could**: Genesis (ii. 27) "So God created man in his own image, in the image of God created He him."

118, 119. **For Love doth...bee**: Cp. the *Timaeus*. "Let me tell you then why the creator created and made the universe. He was good, and no goodness can ever have any jealousy of anything. And being free from jealousy he desired that all things should be as like himself as possible."

120—175. (Man was no less ungrateful than the angels. He also fell from grace and would have totally perished had not the Son of God offered to redeem him. He permitted himself to be born in human shape and crucified to atone for the guilt of man. This death has provided the means of redemption for all mankind and is the most glorious possible example of love.)

121. **whom he did ensew**: whom he followed. Cp. *F. Q.* III. i. 45:

> "And next to him Jocanté did ensew."

126. **Of never-dead...paine**. Pain which is as great as that of death but which never ceases.

128. **Made of meere love**: made out of pure love.

130. **despeyred hell**: hell where there is no hope of release.
The idea is the same as Dante's (*Inferno* III.)

> "Per me si va nella città dolente,
> Pe me si va nell' eterno dolore...
> Lasciate ogni speranza voi ch' entrate."

131. **in doole**: dole or grief (French).

lenger. In A.-S. this adj. was compared by mutation: *lang, lengra*, etc. The change of vowel is one of Spenser's archaisms.

132. **cast**: planned.

136. **demisse**: submissive.

137. **thrall**. Spenser is fond of this word. It is of Scandinavian origin and means 'slave.' It had a flavour of archaism.

138. **sinnes deadly hyre**: "the wages of sin is death."

144. **for mans misguyde**: for man's misguidance. The use of a verb for a noun is frequent in Spenser.

145. **did slyde**: trespass. The image is from slipping or falling on the path.

151. **with despightfull shame**: spite is an abbreviated form of despite. Spenser is fond of the fuller form of the word and it has usually a stronger meaning with him than with us; thus it may mean the extremity of anger. *F. Q.* I. i. 50:

"He thought have slaine her in his fierce despight."

152. **that them most vile became**: that became or suited them most vilely.

153, 154. **At length him...decree.** In identifying Christ as the Just, Spenser was probably thinking of a passage in the *Republic* which was indeed generally considered, like Virgil's hymn, to be an unconscious prophecy of Christ.

Glaucon says (Bk II.): "After describing the men as we have done, there will be no further difficulty, I imagine, in proceeding to sketch the kind of life which awaits them respectively....They will say that in such a situation the just man will be scourged, racked, fettered, will have his eyes burnt out, and at last, after suffering every kind of torture, will be crucified."

153. **gallow-tree**: the wood of a gallows.

158. **launching**: piercing. Cp. *F. Q.* II. i. 38:

"As gentle Hynd, whose sides with cruell steele
Through launched."

160. **Doing him die**: causing him to die. The use of 'do' in this sense is a frequent Spenserian idiom.

161. **heast**: see note on I. 160.

165. **redound**: overflow or abound. Cp. *F. Q.* I. iii. 8:

"Redounding teares did choke th' end of her plaint."

167. **infected cryme**: infixed or inherent (a Latinism).

173. **before all worlds behight**: more than all the promise o₁ the world. Cp. *F. Q.* IV. xi. 6:

"And for his paines a whistle him behight."

175. **Or what can prize that**: what can estimate at its true value.

176—217. (In return for this divine love men are asked to perform but little: they are asked only to love their Deliverer and their fellows who have been redeemed at the same price, they are commanded also to show mercy inasmuch as it has been shown to them.)

176. **in lieu of**: in return for.

177. **for guerdon**: as a reward.

178. **what can us...behove?** how can we possibly owe less than that?

179. **againe:** in return for.

181, 182. He gave us life and restored it when it had been lost; life, of so little value to us, is the least return we can make to him.

184. **that was band:** that was bound.

184—187. The same word can be used as a rhyme when it is employed in different senses or as different parts of speech. This is the Chaucerian rule and it is also Spenser's.

198. **Of that selfe mould.** 'Self' is used as an adjective both by Shakespeare and by Spenser.

"I am made of that self metal as my sister
And prize me at her worth."

(*King Lear* I. i. 70.)

199. Understand **and they**—we and they shall fade again to the same.

200. **like heritage of land:** the grave.

203. Understand **were**.

207. **Which in his...spake:** (John xv. 17) "These things I command you, that ye love one another."

209, 210. **Knowing that, whatsoere...live:** (Matthew xxv. 37—40) "Then shall the righteous answer him, saying, Lord, when saw we thee an hungred, and fed thee? or thirsty, and gave thee drink?"

"And the King shall answer and say unto them, Verily I say unto you, Inasmuch as ye have done it unto one of the least of these my brethren, ye have done it unto me."

211. **reede:** counsel (A.-S. rāed).

213. **ensampled it:** give an example.

218—245. (The poet calls upon the earth to remember the story of its Redeemer. He recalls the life of Christ, His birth, His many sorrows, His crucifixion.)

219. **like to filthy swyne.** The reader should compare the description of the men in Acrasia's bower who have wallowed in sensual pleasures and so been changed into hogs (*F. Q.* II. xii).

220. **moyle:** defile.

222. **eyne:** a weak plural. A.-S. 'eagan.'

226. **cratch:** rack or crib.

230. **silly Shepheards:** innocent or happy. A.-S. 'saelig,' blessed.

68 THE FOWRE HYMNES

231. **Whom greatest Princes sought**: the three Magi who, according to their legend, were eastern kings.

234. **cancred foes**: obstinate or bitter. A word of which Spenser is fond.

> "That conning Architect of cancred guyle."
>
> *(F. Q.* II. i. 1.)

235. **his sharpe assayes**: trials or temptations.

238. **being malist**: treated with malice.

> "From malicing, or grudging his good houre."
>
> *(F. Q.* VI. x. 39.)

239. **of most wretched wights**: by people miserable because they are wretched.

246—287. (The sufferings of Christ should awaken pity and compassion in all who regard them. The author exhorts the reader to love Christ with all his heart and soul and give up all other loves for His sake; he will feel himself inspired and possessed by love, he will no longer desire anything but the celestial beauty he perceives and will see and rejoice in the pure glory of God.)

247. **remorse**: feeling or emotion. This is also a Shakespearean use of the word.

253. **with sence whereof**: *i.e.* of Christ's sufferings.

256. **weale**: happiness or good. The same sense still survives in 'commonweal.'

261. **his beheasts embrace**: obey his commands.

267—287. These stanzas are a paraphrase of the *Symposium* (210, 211).

ὃς γὰρ ἂν μέχρι ἐνταῦθα πρὸς τὰ ἐρωτικὰ παιδαγωγηθῇ, θεώμενος ἐφεξῆς τε καὶ ὀρθῶς τὰ καλά, πρὸς τέλος ἤδη ἰὼν τῶν ἐρωτικῶν ἐξαίφνης κατόψεταί τι θαυμαστὸν τὴν φύσιν καλόν, τοῦτο ἐκεῖνο, οὗ δὴ ἕνεκεν καὶ οἱ ἔμπροσθεν πάντες πόνοι ἦσαν, πρῶτον μὲν ἀεὶ ὂν καὶ οὔτε γιγνόμενον οὔτε ἀπολλύμενον, οὔτε αὐξανόμενον οὔτε φθῖνον, ἔπειτα οὐ τῇ μὲν καλόν, τῇ δ' αἰσχρόν, οὐδὲ τοτὲ μέν, τοτὲ δ' οὔ, οὐδὲ πρὸς μὲν τὸ καλόν, πρὸς δὲ τὸ αἰσχρόν, οὐδ' ἔνθα μὲν καλόν, ἔνθα δὲ αἰσχρόν....ἀλλὰ αὐτὸ καθ' αὑτὸ μεθ' αὑτοῦ μονοειδὲς ἀεὶ ὄν, τὰ δὲ ἄλλα πάντα καλὰ ἐκείνου μετέχοντα τρόπον τινὰ τοιοῦτον, οἷον γιγνομένων τε τῶν ἄλλων καὶ ἀπολλυμένων μηδὲν ἐκεῖνο μήτε τι πλέον μήτε ἔλαττον γίγνεσθαι μηδὲ πάσχειν μηδέν. ...τί δῆτα, ἔφη, οἰόμεθα, εἴ τῳ γένοιτο αὐτὸ τὸ καλὸν ἰδεῖν εἰλικρινές, καθαρόν, ἄμεικτον, ἀλλὰ μὴ ἀνάπλεων σαρκῶν τε ἀνθρωπίνων καὶ χρωμάτων καὶ ἄλλης πολλῆς φλυαρίας θνητῆς, ἀλλ' αὐτὸ τὸ θεῖον καλὸν δύναιτο μονοειδὲς κατιδεῖν. (See also Introduction I.)

279. **passing light**: surpassing.

283, 284. And thy bright...still : *Symposium* 211 :

τοῦτο γὰρ δή ἐστι τὸ ὀρθῶς ἐπὶ τὰ ἐρωτικὰ ἰέναι ἢ ὑπ' ἄλλου ἄγεσθαι,
ἀρχόμενον ἀπὸ τῶνδε τῶν καλῶν ἐκείνου ἕνεκα τοῦ καλοῦ ἀεὶ ἐπανιέναι,
ὥσπερ ἐπαναβαθμοῖς χρώμενον....ὡς ἀπὸ τῶν μαθημάτων ἐπ' ἐκεῖνο τὸ
μάθημα τελευτήσῃ, ὅ ἐστιν οὐκ ἄλλου ἢ αὐτοῦ ἐκείνου τοῦ καλοῦ μάθημα,
καὶ γνῷ αὐτὸ τελευτῶν ὅ ἐστι καλόν.

286. enragement : passion.

HYMN IV.

1—21. (Introduction. The poet has contemplated divine images
of beauty but has no power of expressing the marvels he has seen. He
calls on the Holy Spirit to aid him that he may give men some
conception of this divine beauty so that their minds may be transported
with the sight and they may behold the divine beauty in itself.)

The idea in this passage comes from the *Phaedrus* and *Symposium*
(Introduction II.).

2, 3. Through contemplation of...wrought. *Phaedrus* 249,
250 :

ἔστι δὴ οὖν δεῦρο ὁ πᾶς ἥκων λόγος περὶ τῆς τετάρτης μανίας—ἣν ὅταν
τὸ τῇδέ τις ὁρῶν κάλλος, τοῦ ἀληθοῦς ἀναμιμνησκόμενος, πτερῶταί τε καὶ
ἀναπτερούμενος προθυμούμενος ἀναπτέσθαι, ἀδυνατῶν δέ, ὄρνιθος δίκην
βλέπων ἄνω, τῶν κάτω δὲ ἀμελῶν, αἰτίαν ἔχει ὡς μανικῶς διακείμενος—ὡς
ἄρα αὕτη πασῶν τῶν ἐνθουσιάσεων ἀρίστη τε καὶ ἐξ ἀρίστων τῷ τε ἔχοντι
καὶ τῷ κοινωνοῦντι αὐτῆς γίγνεται, καὶ ὅτι ταύτης μετέχων τῆς μανίας ὁ
ἐρῶν τῶν καλῶν ἐραστὴς καλεῖται. καθάπερ γὰρ εἴρηται, πᾶσα μὲν
ἀνθρώπου ψυχὴ φύσει τεθέαται τὰ ὄντα, ἢ οὐκ ἂν ἦλθεν εἰς τόδε τὸ ζῷον ·
ἀναμιμνήσκεσθαι δ' ἐκ τῶνδε ἐκεῖνα οὐ ῥάδιον ἁπάσῃ, οὔτε ὅσαι βραχέως
εἶδον τότε τἀκεῖ, οὔθ' αἱ δεῦρο πεσοῦσαι ἐδυστύχησαν, ὥστε ὑπό τινων
ὁμιλιῶν ἐπὶ τὸ ἄδικον τραπόμεναι λήθην ὧν τότε εἶδον ἱερῶν ἔχειν.

5. high conceipted sprights : as explained in the passage quoted
above only the noble souls can see the true beauty.

6. I faine to tell : I wish to tell.

7. to fold : to be folded or restrained.

14. distraughted : distracted.

22—63. (The true order of proceeding in matters of beauty is to
begin with this lower world, to admire the beauties revealed in it and
so to proceed to the contemplation of heavenly beauty. The poet

reflects on the wonders of the universe, the earth, the air and other elements, of the heavenly bodies and stars.)

22—28. *Symposium* 210: δεῖ γάρ, ἔφη, τὸν ὀρθῶς ἰόντα ἐπὶ τοῦτο τὸ πρᾶγμα ἄρχεσθαι μὲν νέον ὄντα ἰέναι ἐπὶ τὰ καλὰ σώματα, καὶ πρῶτον μέν, ἐὰν ὀρθῶς ἡγῆται ὁ ἡγούμενος, ἑνὸς αὐτῶν σώματος ἐρᾶν καὶ ἐνταῦθα γεννᾶν λόγους καλούς, ἔπειτα δὲ αὐτὸν κατανοῆσαι, ὅτι τὸ κάλλος τὸ ἐπὶ ὁτῳοῦν σώματι τῷ ἐπὶ ἑτέρῳ σώματι ἀδελφόν ἐστι, καὶ εἰ δεῖ διώκειν τὸ ἐπ' εἴδει καλόν, πολλὴ ἄνοια μὴ οὐχ ἕν τε καὶ ταὐτὸν ἡγεῖσθαι τὸ ἐπὶ πᾶσιν τοῖς σώμασι κάλλος· τοῦτο δ' ἐννοήσαντα καταστῆναι πάντων τῶν καλῶν σωμάτων ἐραστήν, ἑνὸς δὲ τὸ σφόδρα τοῦτο χαλάσαι καταφρονήσαντα καὶ σμικρὸν ἡγησάμενον.

From the love of fair forms generally he will proceed to the love of fair minds, from them to sciences and institutions, and will not be like a slave or small minded man in love with one thing only, but will proceed to the great ocean of beauty beyond:

δουλεύων φαῦλος ᾖ καὶ σμικρολόγος, ἀλλ' ἐπὶ τὸ πολὺ πέλαγος τετραμμένος τοῦ καλοῦ καὶ θεωρῶν πολλοὺς καὶ καλοὺς λόγους καὶ μεγαλοπρεπεῖς τίκτῃ καὶ διανοήματα ἐν φιλοσοφίᾳ ἀφθόνῳ, ἕως ἂν ἐνταῦθα ῥωσθεὶς καὶ αὐξηθεὶς κατίδῃ τινὰ ἐπιστήμην μίαν τοιαύτην, ἥ ἐστι καλοῦ τοιοῦδε....

The parallel is by no means exact, for Plato is speaking of human forms, but the manner of proceeding from stage to stage is the same (see Introduction II.).

26. **the soare faulcon**: a young falcon, or falcon of the first year.

27, 28. She flags or pauses awhile beneath her fluttering wings until she can take breath for stronger flights.

29. **gazefull**: intent or eager.

33. **much lesse their natures aime**: much less the purpose for which they are intended.

36. **on adamantine pillers**: firm foundations.

37. **engirt with brasen bands**: fixed in its place.

38. **still flitting**: always moving.

39. **pyles of flaming brands**: the sphere of 'aether' or fire which, being lighter than air was above and outside it. This arrangement of the elements is according to the general mediaeval belief. So Dante passes from the terrestrial Paradise through the sphere of fire.

41. **that mightie shining christall wall**: the sphere of the fixed stars.

51. **still moving Masse.** Spenser accepts the Ptolemaic astronomy

according to which the sphere of the fixed stars is itself in motion and
turns round its axis once in twenty-four hours.

54. **Whereof each other...passe:** surpassing one another in bright-
ness: not a logical statement.

64—75. We may compare this passage with Plato's *Republic*
(Bk VII.):

"Since this fretted sky is still a part of the visible world, we are
bound to regard it, though the most beautiful and perfect of visible
things, as far inferior nevertheless to those true revolutions, which real
velocity, and real slowness, existing in true number, and in all true
forms, accomplish relatively to each other, carrying with them all that
they contain: which are verily apprehensible by reason and thought,
but not by sight."

64—105. (Fair as the visible things of earth are, the invisible things
in the heavens are fairer still. The heavens which are above the visible
one are yet fairer than it, they rise by degrees increasing in beauty till
they arrive at the empyrean or heaven of heavens, which is the highest
of all: yet the beauty of God surpasses even that of the highest heaven.)

This also is the common mediaeval conception, though Spenser has
developed it in his own way. We find in Dante's *Paradiso* the same
scheme of one heaven succeeding to another, continually increasing in
light, in beauty and in happiness.

71. **these heavens:** the visible ones. Spenser's meaning here is
not quite clear. Dante places one heaven, the lowest, in the moon,
another in the sun, others in the planets, and so by degrees arrives at the
empyrean on which all the others depend. Spenser gives no exact
location but speaks indefinitely of visible and invisible heavens without
stating how many there are or where they are situated.

72. **their first Movers bound:** 'the primum mobile,' whose motion
is communicated directly by divine influence and which carries round
with it the sphere of the fixed stars and all the other spheres within.

75. **redound:** excel or surpass. See note on III. 165.

78. **Faire is the...place.** Dante does not limit the souls of the
blessed to one heaven but distributes them according to their attainment
of virtue.

82—84. **More faire is...inspyred.** This piece of Platonism has
a curious incongruity with the mediaevalism of the rest. The ideas
alluded to are those of Beauty, Temperance, Justice, Wisdom, etc.

Phaedrus 247: ἐν δὲ τῇ περιόδῳ καθορᾷ μὲν αὐτὴν δικαιοσύνην,
καθορᾷ δὲ σωφροσύνην, καθορᾷ δὲ ἐπιστήμην, οὐχ ᾗ γένεσις πρόσεστιν, οὐδ'

ἤ ἐστίν που ἑτέρα ἐν ἑτέρῳ οὖσα ὧν ἡμεῖς νῦν ὄντων καλοῦμεν, ἀλλὰ τὴν ἐν τῷ ὅ ἐστιν ὂν ὄντως ἐπιστήμην οὖσαν.

84. **And pure Intelligences from God inspyred.** Spenser may be referring to the minds or souls which survey the 'ideas' and which have not yet been born into human form. Plato speaks of the divine intelligence (θεοῦ διάνοια) which feeds upon reality.

86. **Powres and mightie Potentates:** two of the angelic orders whose function was to watch over princes and kingdoms.

90. **Dominations:** another of the angelic orders.

91. **fet:** fetched or derived.

93. **with golden wings:** the Cherubim are the angels of contemplation and are represented as coloured blue in old paintings. Spenser only follows tradition when he pleases.

overdight: covered over.

94. **eternall burning Seraphins:** the Seraphim were the angels of love and are represented in mediaeval art with the colour of flame or crimson. Spenser is quite right in ascribing 'fierie light' to them.

99—105. Compare Ficino (II. 4): "Ejus (Deus) gratia omnia: ipse causa est pulchrorum omnium, Quasi dicat, ideo circa regem omnia sunt, quia ad illum tanquam ad finem pro natura sua omnia revolvuntur, quemadmodum ab illo tanquam principio producta sunt omnia."

108. **utmost parts:** outermost.

113—147. (The beauties of earth only serve to remind us feebly of the far greater beauty and splendour of God. Man could not support the sight of the divine beauty and therefore, in the works of God, has a means lent him of approaching it by degrees. Even in his utmost exaltation, however, he should approach with reverence.)

113—119. See Bruno (p. 646): "La è oggetto finale, ultimo et perfettissimo: non gia in questo stato dove non possemo veder dio se non come in ombra et specchio; et peró non ne puo esser oggetto se non in qualche similitudine, non tale qual possa esser abstratta et acquistata da la bellezza et eccellenza corporea per virtú del senso : ma quel puó esser formata nella mente per virtú de l' intelletto."

120—133. See Bruno (246): "Hor di queste specie et similitudini si pasce l' intelletto humano da questo mondo inferiore, sin tanto che non gli sia lecito de mirar con piu puri occhi la bellezza della divinitade. ...Ecco dumque come é differenza in questo stato dove veggiamo la divina bellezza in specie intelligibili tolte da gl' effetti, opre, magisteri, ombre et similitudini di quella, et in quell' altro stato dove sia lecito di vederla in propria presenza."

And Bruno (641—2) : " Ma é un calor acceso dal sole intelligentiale ne l' anima et impeto divino che gl' impronta l' ali, onde piu et piu avvicinandosi al sole intelligentiale, rigettando la ruggine de le humane cure, dovien un oro probato et puro, há sentimento della divina et interna harmonia, concorda gli suoi pensieri et gesti con la simmetria della legge insita in tutte le cose."

We may compare also with Dante (*Paradiso* I.):

> " La gloria di Colui che tutto move
> Per l' universo penetra, e risplende
> In una parte più, e meno altrove."

122. **rebutted backe**: cast back again, *i.e.* we can only bear to see the sun's beams in reflection.

130. **as in a brasen booke**: as in something indelible.

131. **every nooke**: every part or portion; not used quite correctly.

134. **perfect speculation**: the true power of thought.

135. **To impe**: to engraft upon or insert in. The noun 'imp' originally meant a graft or shoot.

137. **damps** : mists or vapours.

148—224. (The poet celebrates the infinite glory and splendour of the Deity, the light in which He dwells and the beauty of His wisdom.)

148. **his mercie seate.** There is no 's' inflexion for the genitive. In A.-S. feminine nouns took a genitive in 'e,' and in M. E. this became blent with any preceding vowel : in Chaucer we have 'Nonnë preestes,' 'lady grace,' etc. In Spenser this usage is an archaism.

151. **That sits** : strictly speaking there is no antecedent for ' that,' but the meaning is plain though the grammar is not.

155. **His scepter is the rod of Righteousnesse**: cp. Psalm xlv. 6 : "The sceptre of thy kingdom is a right sceptre," and Psalm ix. 8, "And he shall judge the world in righteousness."

157. **And the great Dragon strongly doth represse.** The dragon is sin, the slaying of the dragon is the task of the Red Cross Knight. There is a long description of him (*F. Q.* 1. xi. 8—14).

159. **His seate is Truth, to which the faithfull trust**: Psalm cix. 100 : "Thy word is true from the beginning; and every one of thy righteous judgments endureth for ever."

162—168. Cp. Ficino (II. 2): " Sol profecto corpora visibilia et oculos vidientes procreat : oculis ut videant lucidum infundit spiritum :

corpora ut videantur coloribus pingit. Neque tamen proprius oculis radius, propriique corporibus colores ad visionem perficiendam sufficiunt, nisi lumen ipsum unum supra multa, à quo multa et propria lumina oculis et corporibus distributa sunt, adveniat, illustret, excitet atque roboret....Sed divini solis perpetua et invisibilis lux una semper omnibus adstat, fovet, vivificat, excitat, et complet."

169—175. Cp. Ficino (VI. 17): "Tolle postremo diversarum illum numerum idearum, unam simplicem ac meram relinque lucem : instar lucis ejus, quae in globo solis ipso permanet, per aerem non dispergitur : iam Dei pulchritudinem quodammodo comprehendis, quae tantum saltem formas reliquas antecellit, quantum lux illa solis in seipsa mera, una, inviolata, splendorem solis per nubilosum aera disjectum, divisum, insectum, obscuratum exuperat. Fons itaque totius pulchritudinis Deus est."

165. **are red**: are interpreted or understood.

175. **Through heavenly vertue**: through heavenly power.

178. **hid in his owne brightnesse from the sight.** Cp. *Paradise Lost* III. 377—380:

> "Amidst the glorious brightness where thou sitt'st
> Throned inaccessible...
> Dark with excessive bright thy skirts appear."

180—182. **And underneath his...yre.** Cp. *Paradise Lost* III. 392—394:

> "Thou that day
> Thy Father's dreadful thunder didst not spare
> Nor stop thy flaming chariot wheels."

183—224. There is a good deal of Catholicism still remaining in Spenser and nowhere is it more curiously represented than here. The description of Wisdom, or Sapience, as the most beautiful of the ideas is to be found in the *Phaedrus* (see Introduction II.), but Spenser gives her exactly the place and prominence in heaven which Catholic writers gave the Virgin Mary, and he attributes to her precisely the same qualities of personal beauty, declaring her to excel Venus in loveliness.

The foundation for the passage is to be found in *Phaedrus* 250 :

ὄψις γὰρ ἡμῖν ὀξυτάτη τῶν διὰ τοῦ σώματος ἔρχεται αἰσθήσεων, ᾗ φρόνησις οὐχ ὁρᾶται—δεινοὺς γὰρ ἂν παρεῖχεν ἔρωτας, εἴ τι τοιοῦτον ἑαυτῆς ἐναργὲς εἴδωλον παρείχετο εἰς ὄψιν ἰόν—καὶ τἆλλα ὅσα ἐραστά.

183. **Sapience**: "φρόνησις."

184. **The soveraine dearling**: the best beloved.

189—210. We may compare this with Dante's hymn to the Virgin (*Paradiso* XXXIII.):

> "Vergine madre, figlia del tuo Figlio,...
> Termine fisso d' eterno consiglio,...
> In te misericordia, in te pietate,
> In te magnificenza, in te s' aduna
> Quantunque in creatura è di bontate."

190. **a crowne of purest gold**: Sapience is crowned like the Virgin. (The Coronation of the Virgin is one of the favourite subjects of Italian art.)

211—214. **Ne could that...skill.** The reference, as the next stanza suggests, is probably to Anacreon (*Ode* 56), who describes a marvellous painting representing Venus in all her beauty floating on the sea.

212. **with so curious quill**: 'curious'—elaborate or wonderful.

quill: a general term for the pencil or brush.

216. **fabling wits**: the writers of fables or poets.

219. **Teian Poet**: Anacreon.

223. **Idole of his fayning thought**: Venus or Aphrodite. This thought of her is said to be 'fayning' because she existed only in his imagination.

224. **be fraught**: filled or laden.

225—301. (Sapience or Wisdom is of an incomparable beauty. She can bestow greater happiness upon man than it is possible for him to attain in any other way; few are worthy of being received into her divine presence, but those whom she does admit are transported with infinite delight. They see such things that they are filled with ecstasy; henceforth they can no longer think of earthly pleasures. The poet exhorts his soul to regard earthly beauty no longer which is but a shadow and to look upon the beauty which is divine.)

The description of the way in which Sapience can reward those who truly love, again bears the closest resemblance to the Catholic descriptions of the Virgin.

Spenser, however, concludes by identifying his Sapience with perfect beauty, and his account of the absolute rapture and contentment of beholding this is again taken from the *Symposium*. (See Introduction II.)

225. **the novice of his Art**: an unskilled poet.

227. **her least perfections part**: the least part of her perfection.

231. **so heavenly hew**: such a heavenly shape or form. A.-S. 'hiw.'

235. that faire love of mightie heavens King : the beloved of the King, *i.e.* Sapience.

246—252. The idea of Sapience as a kind of intermediary between God and man recalls the position ascribed to the Virgin. We may compare Dante (*Paradiso* XXXIII.):

> "Donna, sei tanto grande, e tanto vali,
>> Che qual vuol grazia, ed a te non ricorre,
>> Sua disianza vuol volar senz' ali.
> La tua benignità non pur soccorre
>> A chi demanda, ma molte fiate
>> Liberamente al dimandar precorre."

263. filles the brasen sky: the sky which is fixed or firm.

266—280. We may compare Bruno (p. 672): "Bisogna dumque alzarsi á quello intelletto superiore il quale da per se é bello, et da per se é buono. Questo é quell' unico et supremo capitano, qual solo messo alla presenza de gl' occhi di militanti pensieri, le illustra, incoraggia, rinforza et rende vittoriosi sul dispreggio d' ogn' altra bellezza, et repudio di qualsuogl' altre bene."

274. that faire lampe: beauty.

281—287. Compare Ficino (IV. 4): "Solus deus cui deest nihil, supra quem nihil, seipso contentus permanet, sibi sufficiens, quapropter deo se parem fecit tunc animus, cum se solo voluit esse contentus, quasi non minus quam deus sibi esse sufficeret."

286. fastened mynd: firmly fixed or steadfast.

293. through thy follies prief: through the fruit of thy folly.

294. on matter of thy grief: that which has only given grief.

INDEX.

Achilles in Homer xii; in *Symposium* xliii; in Spenser xliii, 49, 50

Aeneas 50

Agathon xlvii: see *Symposium*

Alkestis in *Symposium* xliii; in Spenser 49

Anacreon 75

Aphrodite xlv, xlviii

Apologie for Poetrie see Sidney

Aristophanes xlvi, xlvii; see *Symposium*

Aristotle, influence of ix, x; ethics of xvi; temperance in xviii

Atlantis xiv

Bessarion x

Boethius ix

Bruno Giordano x; influence of on *Fowre Hymnes* lviii—lxxii; see also *Heroici Furori De gl'*

Cabala x

Cambridge at Reformation x

Charmides xiii

Chaucer 61

Commentarium in Convivium x; influence of on *Fowre Hymnes* lviii—lxxii; quotations from in original lx, lxii, lxvii, lxix—lxx, 45—47, 55—61, 72—74, 76

Critias xvii

Dante ix, xxxviii, lv, 57, 70—71; quotations from 65, 73, 75—76

Diotima of Mantineia xlviii—lii; see speech of Socrates in *Symposium*

Eryximachus xlv; see *Symposium*

Faerie Queene see Spenser

Ficino Marsilio position in Renaissance x; speech of Eryximachus in xlv; speech of Aristophanes in xlvi; speech of Agathon in xlvii; influence of on *Fowre Hymnes* lviii—lxxii; see also *Commentarium in Convivium*

Fowre Hymnes, Platonism in xii; date of writing xiv; publication of xxviii; alterations in xxviii; influence of *Phaedrus* on xxxv—xli; influence of *Symposium* on xli—lv; influence of *Timaeus* on lvi; influ-

ence of Bruno and Ficino on
lviii—lxxii ; stanza of 43

Hebe 52
Hercules 52
Heroici Furori De gl' influence
of on *Fowre Hymnes* lviii—
lxxii ; quotations from in ori-
ginal lxiii—lxv, lxxi—lxxii, 51,
55—58, 60—61, 72—73, 76
Hesiod xli
Homer xii

Laches, theory of virtue in xvi,
xix
Lucretius 53

Mary, Virgin xl, 74—76
Meno, doctrine of recollection in
xxix
Milton 54, 64, 74

Neo-Platonism ix, x

Orpheus xliii, 49—50

Parmenides, doctrine of ideas in
xxx
Pater xi, xiii
Pausanias xliv—xlv ; see *Sym-
posium*
Petrarch ix
Phaedo xv
Phaedrus xii ; allegory in xiv ;
virtue in xiv ; influence on
Faerie Queene xviii—xxi ; sum-
mary of xxix—xxxv ; influence
of on *Fowre Hymnes* xxxv—
xli ; quotations from original
xxx—xxxiv, 47—48, 52, 59,
62, 69, 71, 74 ; speech of
Phaedrus in *Symposium* xxxiii

Philo x
Plato : Platonism in Italy ix, x,
xii ; Plato and the Reforma-
tion x ; allegory in xii ; Pla-
tonism in Spenser xi ; function
of poetry according to xiii ;
narrative in xiii ; influence of
on *Faerie Queene* xiv—xxiii ;
influence of on Spenser's *Minor
Poems* xxiii—xxviii ; Platonists,
Italian xxix ; see also *Phae-
drus, Symposium, Timaeus,
Republic,* etc.
Plethon, Gemistus ix, x
Plotinus x, lviii
Puritanism xi

Ramus x
Republic xii ; theory of poetry
in xiii ; allegory in xiv ; virtue
in xv ; psychology in xvi ;
ethics of xvii ; justice in xxii ;
just man in xxiii, 66 ; influ-
ence of on *Fowre Hymnes*
lvii ; heaven in 71

Shakespeare xxv
Shelley ix
Sidney, Sir Philip xiii, xxv,
lviii
Socrates : in *Republic* xii ; as
righteousness xiii ; in *Phaedo*
xv ; in *Laches* xvi, xix ; death
of xvii ; wisdom of xvii ; see
also *Phaedrus* and *Symposium*
Spenser, Edmund : Puritanism
and Platonism in xi ; *Minor
Poems* of : *Shepheards Calender*
xi, xiv ; *Colin Clout's Come
Home Againe* xxiv ; *Teares of
the Muses* xxiii ; *Epithalamium*
xxv ; *Sonnets* xxv—xxviii, 44 ;

Faerie Queene : moral allegory in xiii ; influence of Plato on xiv—xxiii ; characters in : Alma xvi, xvii ; Amoret xxii, 44, 52; Artegall xiii, xx ; Britomart xiii, xviii, xix—xxi ; Busirane xviii; Calidore xxiii ; Despair xv ; Florimell xxii ; Guyon xiii, xvi—xvii, xxiii ; Malbecco 52 ; Pastorella xxiii ; Satyrane xv ; Scudamour xxii, 44, 52—53; Una xiv ; places in : House of Holiness xv—xvi ; Cave of Mammon xvi—xvii ; Acrasia's Bower xvi, 53 ; House of Temperance xvii ; Gardens of Venus xxiii ; quotations from xv, xvii—xxii, 49, 52, 64 ; influence of Bruno on lviii

Symposium xii ; influence on *Faerie Queene* xv, xviii—xix, xxii ; analysis of xli—lii ; influence of on *Fowre Hymnes* xli—lv ; quotations from original xlii—xliv, xlvii, xlix, 45—47, 50, 59 ; speech of Phaedrus in xli—xliv ; speech of Pausanias in xliv—xlv ; speech of Eryximachus in xlv; speech of Aristophanes in xlvi—xlvii; speech of Agathon in xlvii ; speech of Socrates in xlviii—lii

Timaeus xvi, xvii ; influence of on *Fowre Hymnes* lvi; quotations from 54, 63, 65, 68—70

Uranus xlv

Zeus xlv—xlvi

For EU product safety concerns, contact us at Calle de José Abascal, 56–1°,
28003 Madrid, Spain or eugpsr@cambridge.org.